To my favorite Swiftie!
Much love,
Nana ☺ xoxo

INDEPENDENT AND UNOFFICIAL

POP CULTURE ENCYCLOPEDIAS

Taylor Swift's THE ERAS TOUR ENCYCLOPEDIA

BY MARI BOLTE

Encyclopedias
An Imprint of Abdo Reference
abdobooks.com

TABLE OF CONTENTS

INTRODUCTION 4

THE ERAS TOUR 6
- The Breakdown 8
- The United States Tour 10
- The World Tour 14
- Ticket Sales 18
- Easter Eggs 20
- The Fans 22
- The Supporting Acts 24
- The Merch 26
- The Movie 28
- The Choreographer 30
- The Dancers 32
- The Musicians 36

THE STAGE 38
- The Main Stage 38
- *Lover* 40
- *Fearless* 42
- *evermore* 44
- *Reputation* 46
- *Speak Now* 48
- *Red* 50
- *folklore* 52
- *1989* 54
- Surprise Songs 56
- *Midnights* 58

THE COSTUMES **60**
   Lover 60
   Fearless 66
   evermore 70
   Reputation 74
   Speak Now 76
   Red 86
   folklore 92
   1989 100
   Surprise Songs 104
   Midnights 108

THE SET LIST **116**
   Lover 116
   Fearless 124
   evermore 130
   Reputation 138
   Speak Now 144
   Red 148
   folklore 156
   1989 166
   Surprise Songs 174
   Midnights 178

GLOSSARY **188**
TO LEARN MORE **189**
INDEX **190**
PHOTO CREDITS **191**

INTRODUCTION

Taylor Swift is a singer-songwriter, producer, business woman, and director. She is one of the world's best-selling artists, filling stadiums around the globe on every tour.

Swift began performing at a young age. By the time she was 13, her family moved from Pennsylvania to Tennessee, hoping to get Swift signed by a record label. Signing with a label is a big deal. Record labels help artists reach more people by marketing their recordings.

In 2004, Swift signed with Sony/ATV. She was just 14 years old. But soon after, she moved to Big Machine Records, headed by an executive named Scott Borchetta. Later, Borchetta would sell the label to Scooter Braun. Swift released her debut album, *Taylor Swift*, in 2006.

In March 2023, Swift announced her first concert tour since 2018. The Eras Tour would be her sixth tour. Millions of fans would get the chance to see their favorite performer live.

In 2023, Swift was the most-streamed artist on Spotify with more than 26.1 billion streams.

THE ERAS TOUR

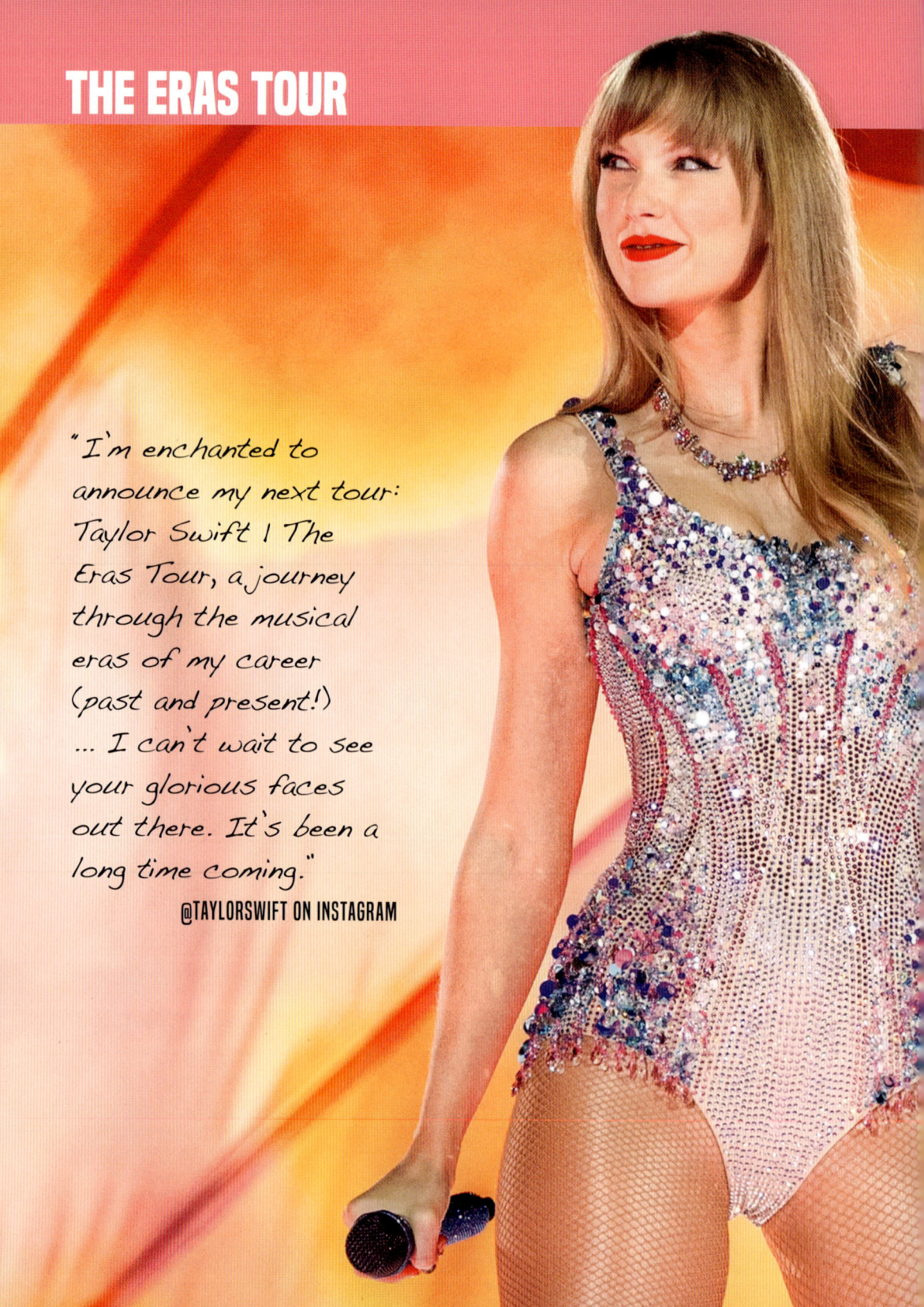

"I'm enchanted to announce my next tour: Taylor Swift | The Eras Tour, a journey through the musical eras of my career (past and present!) ... I can't wait to see your glorious faces out there. It's been a long time coming."

@TAYLORSWIFT ON INSTAGRAM

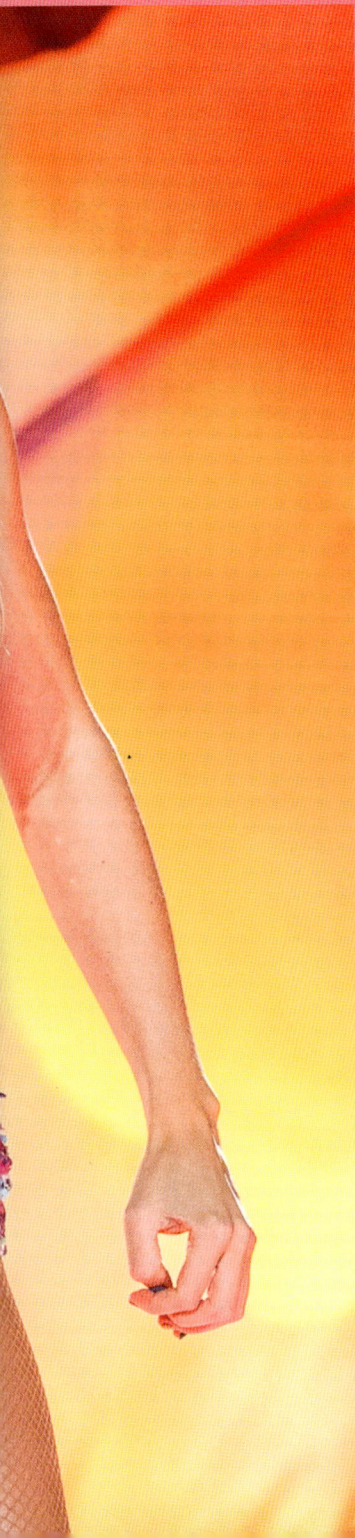

On October 21, 2022, Taylor Swift released her album, *Midnights*. In its first week, it was streamed more than one billion times worldwide. Swift became the first—and only—artist to have five albums sell more than a million units in that time. Her name dominated top 10 lists around the world. No one was hotter than Swift. And then, on November 1, 2022, she announced the biggest event of her career—The Eras Tour.

Fans went wild. Swift hadn't toured since 2018. Swift had 199 songs from 10 albums to choose from. The albums spanned several genres. The singer-songwriter got her start in country music, but she has also explored pop music, folk music, and even alternative rock. Everyone had their favorite track.

Swift had built a visual journey that took fans through nearly 20 years of her music. The Eras Tour concert would be more than a night of music. It would be a theatrical performance, with costume and set changes, epic choreography, surprise songs, and guest stars. The world was ready and waiting.

Taylor Swift was *Time* magazine's 2023 Person of the Year. *Time* said, "This was the year Taylor Swift perfected her craft."

THE ERAS TOUR

THE BREAKDOWN

A select number of fans who had Capital One credit cards or who had been chosen through the Ticketmaster Verified Fan program got access to a presale starting on November 15, 2022. The presale would last until November 17, or "while supplies last." Everyone else would be able to try for tickets starting on November 18.

Supplies didn't last that long. More than 3.5 million people had registered for the presale and more than two million tickets were sold on the first day. Ticketmaster's website crashed over and over, frustrating fans. Even so, millions of fans would get to see their favorite performer.

The tour's unprecedented demand poured money into economies around the United States and the world. Fans spent money not only on tickets, but on travel, hotels, food, and their outfits. In all, the Eras Tour brought an estimated $5.7 billion to the United States economy.

AT A GLANCE

- 152 shows across five continents
- The tour kicked off on March 17, 2023
- Original end date was August 5, 2023
- By November 4, 2022, eight more dates had been announced
- By November 11, another 17 dates had been added

"I'm going to take a wild guess and say that if you're here tonight, there's a pretty good chance that you went to a considerable amount of effort to be with us tonight . . . Thank you from the bottom of our hearts for wanting to be with us on night one."

—TAYLOR SWIFT ON HER OPENING NIGHT

Depending on the section, face value tickets to the Eras Tour cost between $49 and $499 in the US.

FUN FACT
In total, 4.35 million tickets were sold for the first 60 shows.

THE UNITED STATES TOUR

Swift kicked off the Eras Tour in Glendale, Arizona, at State Farm Stadium. More than 69,000 fans were there, making it the most-attended concert by a female artist. Originally, there had only been one show scheduled in Glendale, but a second show was added due to the extreme demand for tickets. The mayor renamed the city Swift City for those two days to celebrate.

Other cities followed suit, giving Swift a key to their city, making her an honorary mayor, and even naming a street after her. Every city with a tour stop celebrated like Swifties too. Pre- and post-show parties, trivia nights, and other special events made out-of-town fans feel welcome.

In 2017, Swift trademarked the word "Swifties."

Swifties are passionate and loyal fans of Taylor Swift.

Swift's influence went even farther than city limits. One airline waived change fees for concertgoers after their show was postponed. Another added 2,000 extra seats to accommodate fans flying in. Hotels and restaurants announced Taylor Swift packages, special food and drinks, and activities such as bracelet- or candle-making.

SWIFTIES SET SAIL

Luxury cruise ships began offering Swift-themed cruises. Cruise names included The Bestie Cruise and In My Cruise Era. Fans met other fans, dressed up in Eras Tour–themed outfits, traded friendship bracelets, sang karaoke, and more.

THE ERAS TOUR

1. Glendale, Arizona
2. Las Vegas, Nevada
3. Arlington, Texas
4. Tampa, Florida
5. Houston, Texas
6. Atlanta, Georgia
7. Nashville, Tennessee
8. Philadelphia, Pennsylvania
9. Foxborough, Massachusetts
10. East Rutherford, New Jersey
11. Chicago, Illinois
12. Detroit, Michigan
13. Pittsburgh, Pennsylvania
14. Minneapolis, Minnesota
15. Cincinnati, Ohio
16. Kansas City, Missouri
17. Denver, Colorado
18. Seattle, Washington
19. Santa Clara, California
20. Los Angeles, California
21. Miami, Florida
22. New Orleans, Louisiana
23. Indianapolis, Indiana

THE WORLD TOUR

The Eras Tour didn't just set records in North America. It set global records too. Swift traveled across Asia, Australia, and Europe, filling soccer, cricket, and baseball stadiums. Tickets to her Sydney shows sold out in 82 minutes. Some fans tried to avoid a repeat of the Ticketmaster incident by waiting in physical lines. They camped out in front of ticket desks in Melbourne and Sydney, lining up the night before sales started.

By December 2023, it was estimated that the Eras Tour had sold $1.04 billion in tickets, setting a Guinness World Record. It was the highest-grossing tour in history and the first time a tour had ever surpassed $1 billion. It was expected that Swift's 2024 sales numbers would be similar.

TOP FIVE CONCERT TOURS OF ALL TIME

Billboard has recorded the biggest tours in the world since the 1980s. Here are the top five grossing tours of all time.

1. **Taylor Swift—Eras Tour**
   Years: 2023 to 2024
   Gross: $1.04 billion
2. **Elton John—Farewell Yellow Brick Road Tour**
   Years: 2018 to 2023
   Gross: $939.1 million
3. **Ed Sheeran—Divide Tour**
   Years: 2017 to 2019
   Gross: $776 million
4. **U2—U2 360° Tour**
   Years: 2009 to 2011
   Gross: $736 million
5. **Coldplay—Music of the Spheres World Tour**
   Years: 2022 to 2023
   Gross: $617.8 million

Swift took care of her tour crew. Bonuses amounting to more than $55 million were given to the entire staff.

THE ERAS TOUR

WORLD TOUR LOCATIONS

1. Mexico City, Mexico
2. Buenos Aires, Argentina
3. Rio de Janeiro, Brazil
4. São Paulo, Brazil
5. Tokyo, Japan
6. Melbourne, Australia
7. Sydney, Australia
8. Singapore, Singapore
9. Paris, France
10. Stockholm, Sweden
11. Lisbon, Portugal
12. Madrid, Spain
13. Lyon, France
14. Edinburgh, Scotland

Europe

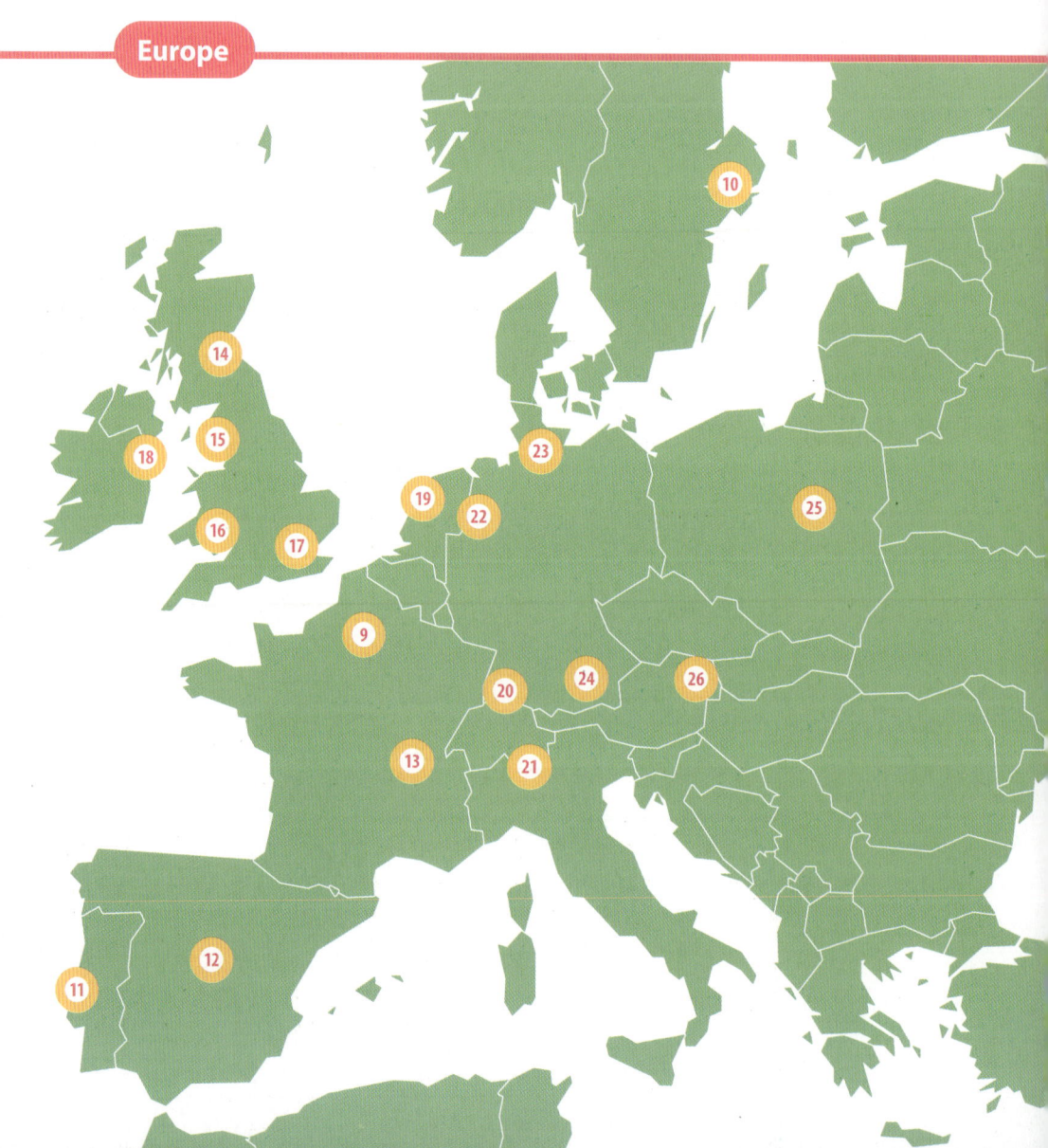

15. Liverpool, England
16. Cardiff, Wales
17. London, England
18. Dublin, Ireland
19. Amsterdam, the Netherlands
20. Zurich, Switzerland
21. Milan, Italy
22. Gelsenkirchen, Germany
23. Hamburg, Germany
24. Munich, Germany
25. Warsaw, Poland
26. Vienna, Austria
27. Toronto, Canada
28. Vancouver, Canada

Asia and the Pacific

Americas

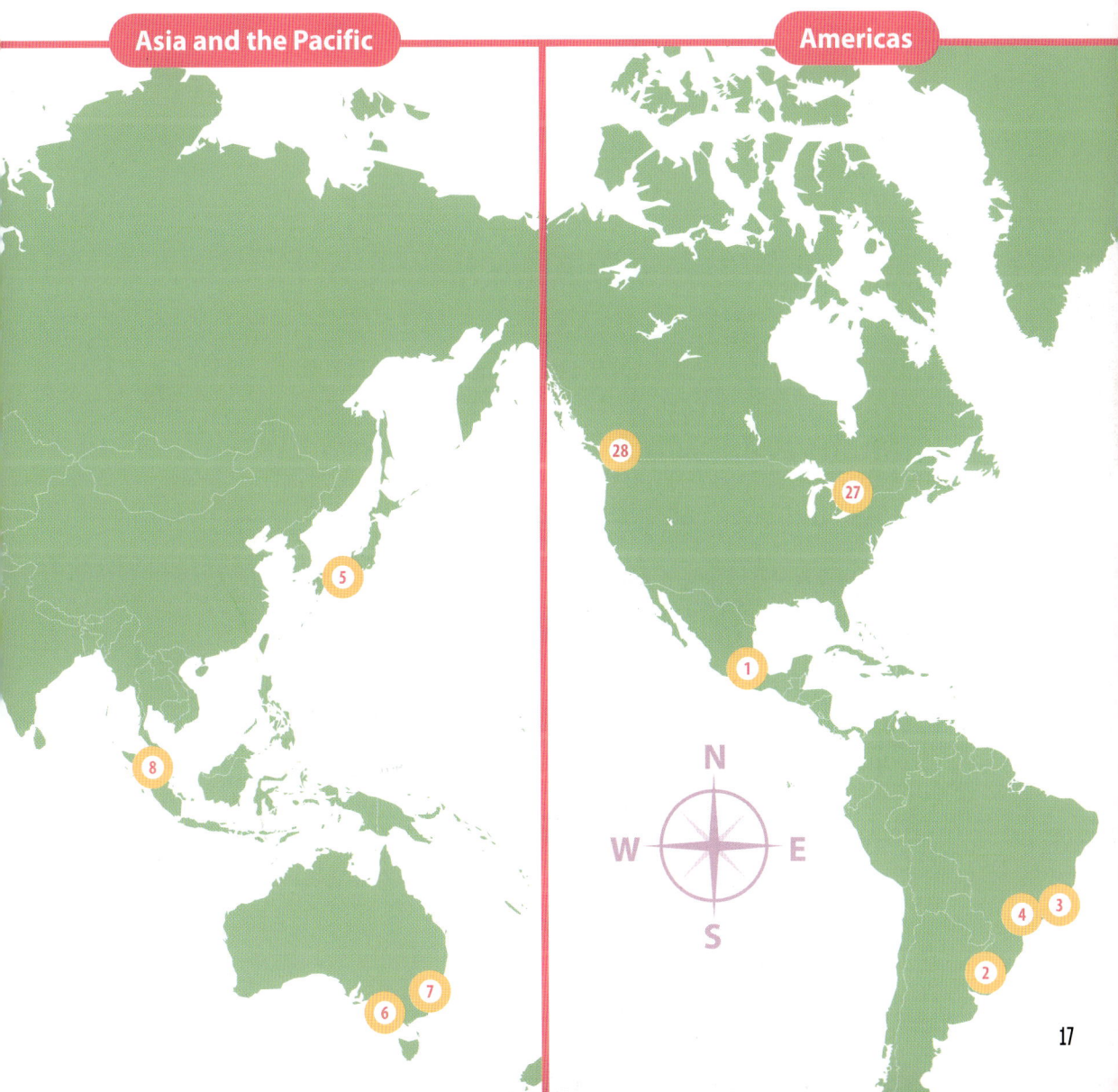

TICKETS SALES

The average ticket price was $253.56, with the cheapest going for $49 and the most expensive at $499. There were also VIP packages as expensive as $899. Packages came with extras such as early access, bags, pins, stickers, lanyards, and prints. The economic impact of a tour stop would be huge. Business owners, local politicians, and even world leaders begged Swift to include their cities.

In Canada, an estimated 31 million people registered for presale in the hopes of getting tickets to one of the six Toronto dates. That was nearly 80% of Canada's entire population. The Rogers Centre, where the concert took place, had a 50,000-seat capacity. Included in the 31 million who had registered were resellers and bots. They listed tickets on resale sites almost immediately. The highest prices ranged anywhere from $17,000 to more than $30,000.

TAYLOR'S VERSION

In 2018, Swift worked to negotiate the ownership of her first six studio albums. The outcome did not meet her professional goals. Instead, she started rerecording her songs in 2021. Her first one, *Fearless (Taylor's Version)*, came out in April 2021. Every album she rereleased hit number 1 on the Billboard 200. Swift was the first living artist in six decades to have four albums on Billboard's Top 10 at the same time. The streaming royalties from the first three rereleased albums made Swift more than $8.5 million per month in 2023.

FUN FACT

It cost $750,000 a day to transport the Eras Tour stage and equipment around the US. The set fit onto 90 semitrucks.

Aside from ticket costs, fans spent an average of $1,300 to attend the concert.

THE ERAS TOUR

EASTER EGGS

Swift has hidden secret messages, clues, and hints in her work throughout her career. These bits of "bonus" content are called Easter eggs. It's an attention to detail that fans love to search for and find. Swift called back some of those details while onstage.

When Swift was in high school, she began making hand hearts to connect with her audience. She said, "It means something between 'I love you' and 'Thank you.'" She still uses the heart-hands symbol to send her message to Swifties.

"I love to communicate through Easter eggs. I think the best messages are cryptic ones."

—SWIFT IN A 2019 INTERVIEW

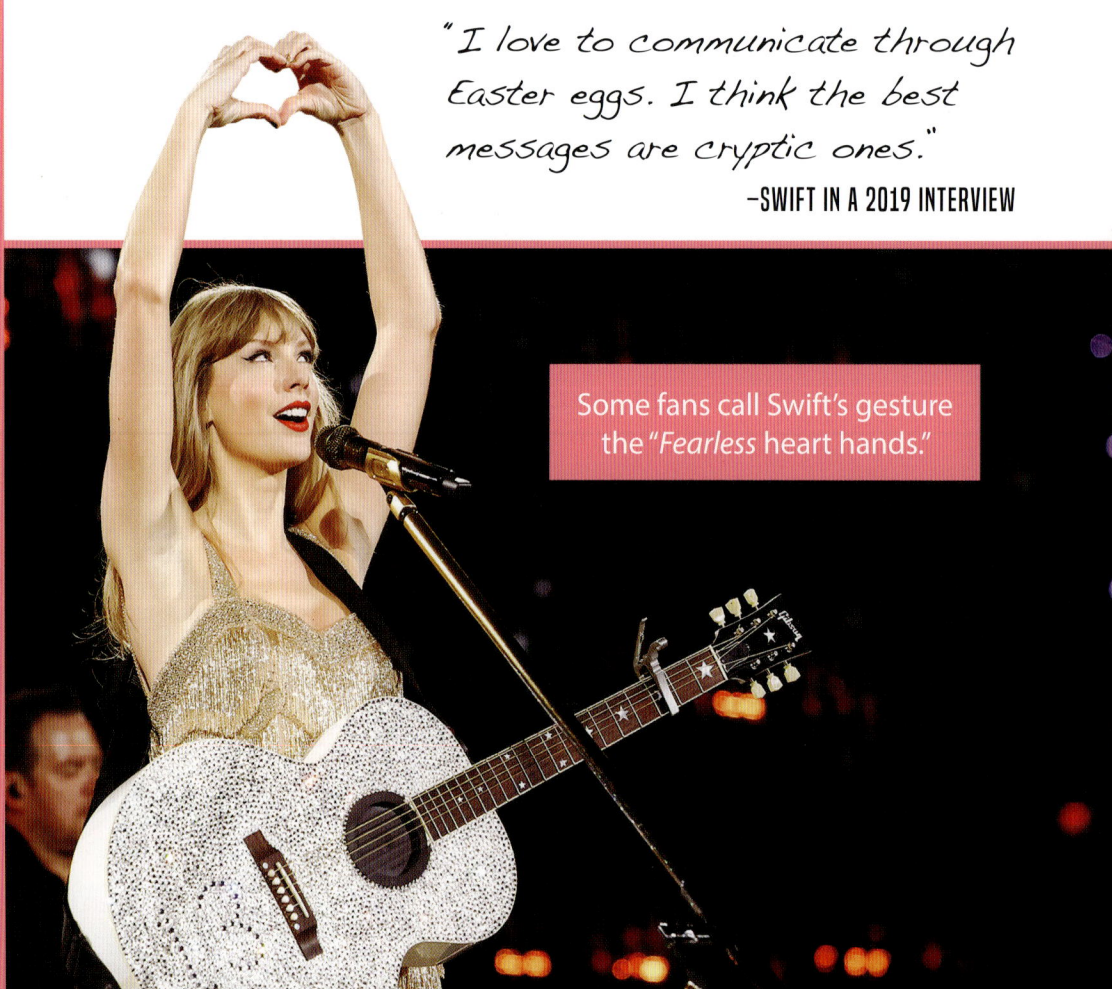

Some fans call Swift's gesture the "*Fearless* heart hands."

The Lover House burning down was a shock to concertgoers.

WHAT ERA IS IT?

Swift's outfits and sets alluded to her 10 albums. Each had its own color palette that fans identified. They even noticed when Swift changed her nail polish shade. Each album is associated with a different color.

Taylor Swift—soft green
Fearless—gold
Speak Now—purple
Red—red
1989—bright blue
Reputation—black
Lover—pastel pink
folklore—gray
evermore—beige
Midnights—dark blue

21

THE FANS

Swifties are one of the largest fan bases in the world. In the past, Swift hosted "Secret Sessions" for die-hard Swifties, flying groups to her homes around the world to hang out. When it comes to their favorite artist, Swifties come out in full force. During her Seattle stops, cheering fans celebrated loud enough to shake the earth as much as a 2.3 magnitude earthquake.

So make the friendship bracelets / Take the moment and taste it / You've got no reason to be afraid

—TAYLOR SWIFT, "YOU'RE ON YOUR OWN, KID"

Swifties used record amounts of data during concerts. They watched and uploaded TikToks, streamed music or videos, and shared Snaps with friends and family who couldn't be there.

One way Swifties identify each other is with friendship bracelets. Trading bracelets with other Swifties, giving them out as gifts, and displaying huge bracelet collections are signs of a true Swiftie. Sales of bracelet-making supplies spiked more than 500 percent after the Eras Tour was announced.

Even famous fans got into the trend. NFL star Travis Kelce made Swift a bracelet for her concerts at Arrowhead Stadium. Movie and music stars such as Jennifer Lawrence, Keith Urban, and Sabrina Carpenter showed off bracelets made by their own fans. Even Swift's personal security guard was spotted with a bracelet around his wrist.

Filipino Swiftie Mikael Arellano created TikTok dances for some of Swift's songs. One of his moves was for "Bejeweled." Hundreds of thousands of people copied his dance to create their own version of the strut. Then Swift did it herself! Arellano was given free concert tickets. On the night he attended, he was steered close to the stage, where Swift held his hand and gave him her "22" hat.

THE SUPPORTING ACTS

Each stop on the Eras Tour had two opening acts, with 10 possible performers. Some performers, such as Paramore and HAIM, had longtime friendships with Swift. Others were newer artists who Swift recognized for their potential. The list of opening acts set an example for supporting women-led and inclusive musicians.

There were also a number of guest appearances, where singers came onstage to duet with Swift during her two surprise songs.

OPENING ACT/FIRST APPEARANCE DATE AND LOCATION

Opening Act	First Appearance	Date and Location
GAYLE	March 17, 2023	State Farm Stadium, Glendale, AZ
Paramore	March 17, 2023	State Farm Stadium, Glendale, AZ
Beabadoobee	March 24, 2023	Allegiant Stadium, Las Vegas, NV
MUNA	March 31, 2023	AT&T Stadium, Arlington, TX
Gracie Abrams	April 1, 2023	AT&T Stadium, Arlington, TX
Phoebe Bridgers	May 5, 2023	Nissan Stadium, Nashville, TN
OWENN	May 28, 2023	MetLife Stadium, East Rutherford, NJ
Girl in Red	June 2, 2023	Soldier Field, Chicago, IL
HAIM	July 22, 2023	Lumen Field, Seattle, WA
Sabrina Carpenter	August 24, 2023	Foro Sol, Mexico City, Mexico

GUEST PERFORMER/SONG(S)

Marcus Mumford	"Cowboy Like Me"
Aaron Dessner	"The Great War"
	"Would've, Could've, Should've"
	"Mad Woman"
Phoebe Bridgers	"Nothing New"
Maren Morris	"You All Over Me"
Jack Antonoff	"Getaway Car"
Ice Spice	"Karma" remix

FUN FACT
During the Kansas City stop, Taylor Lautner, Presley Cash, and Joey King appeared onstage after a surprise premiere of Swift's newest music video, "I Can See You." All three are in the video.

Swift and the Haim sisters became friends in 2014.

THE MERCH

The official Eras Tour store sold apparel, records and CDs, and even accessories such as pillowcases, guitar picks, umbrellas, and jewelry. Knowing not all Swifties were able to get tickets to the show itself, official merchandise trucks were parked in every Eras Tour city the day before each show. Some people waited as long as 11 hours to buy Eras Tour souvenirs. But their waiting paid off. Some exclusive items were only sold at outdoor merch trucks. Others were online only.

Each city on the tour stop had its own personalized poster.

The average Swiftie spent $208 on merchandise.

One of the most sought-after items was a blue crew neck sweater. Resellers were listing it for hundreds of dollars. A deluxe version of *Midnights*, called *Midnights (The Late Night Edition)*, had a never-before-released song, and one not available on streaming services, on its track list. It was only available as a CD and only sold at Swift's New Jersey shows. Only ticketed fans could get a copy.

SELL IT, SWIFTIES

Around $200 million in Eras Tour merchandise was sold from November 17, 2022, to November 15, 2023. That's more than the 10th highest-grossing tour of 2023, Drake's It's All a Blur Tour, made on its ticket sales alone.

THE ERAS TOUR

THE MOVIE

On August 31, 2023, Swift made an announcement that excited her fans. Even people who weren't able to get tickets to the live show could experience the Eras Tour—it was coming to movie theaters around the world! Tickets would cost $19.89 for adults and $13.13 for kids. Special posters, popcorn buckets, drink cups, and other exclusive merchandise were sold at theaters.

Capturing the Taylor Swift experience on film took a lot of work. It was filmed over three days at So-Fi Stadium and cost between $10 and $20 million to make. More than 40 camera operators, as well as drones, GoPros, and Spidercams, were used to capture the action. More than 100 microphones were used to pick up sounds on separate tracks.

Swift surprised fans at *The Eras Tour* World Premiere in Los Angeles, California.

Swift, her dancers, and band attended *Taylor Swift: The Eras Tour* World Premiere on October 11, 2023.

Taylor Swift: The Eras Tour made $123 million during its opening weekend and $250 million at the global box office. It was the highest-grossing concert or performance film of all time. On December 13 (Swift's birthday), it became available on streaming services for a price of $19.89.

THE TOUR AT HOME

The film differed slightly from the live concert. There are no guest appearances in the movie. Six songs were also cut. The streaming release featured three new performances. On March 14, 2024, *The Eras Tour (Taylor's Version)* was released on Disney+. It contained five bonus songs and four acoustic performances. By March 19, it had been watched 4.6 million times, making it the number-one music film ever released on the platform.

THE CHOREOGRAPHER

MANDY MOORE

In the past, Swift's strength was her music, not her choreography. She admitted that learning dance moves was hard for her. But she trained for three months before the Eras Tour. She worked on her cardio, running on a treadmill while singing the entire set list. And she hired a good dance coach to bring her songs to life.

Choreographer Mandy Moore had worked on *Dancing with the Stars* seasons 20 through 25 and had guest judged on season 24. She had also worked on movies and TV shows such as *So You Think You Can Dance* and *La La Land*. Swift hired her to develop all the choreography for the Eras Tour.

Moore broke down each Era like it was a musical. Themed sets, coordinated outfits, and skilled backup dancers turned Swift's music into visual art. The live choreography also coordinated with prerecorded videos of Swift, which were displayed on huge screens alongside the stage.

Moore won a Creative Arts Emmy for her work on *So You Think You Can Dance* in 2018.

FUN FACT
Jeremy Hudson and Amanda Balen were associate choreographers who helped bring the Eras Tour to life. Both were former backup dancers for Lady Gaga.

Moore teaching a dance routine for *So You Think You Can Dance*.

WHAT MORE CAN MOORE DO?

Notable Films, TV Shows, and Venues: *American Idol* (2005-2009), *America's Got Talent* (2008-2017), *So You Think You Can Dance* (2010-2017), *Silver Linings Playbook* (2012), *Dancing with the Stars* (2015-2023), *La La Land* (2016), *Grammy Awards* (2017), *Golden Globe Awards* (2017), *Emmy Awards* (2017, 2018), *Oscars* (2017, 2018), *Zoey's Extraordinary Playlist* (2020-2021)

Notable Awards: Emmy, *Dancing with the Stars* (2017), Emmy, *So You Think You Can Dance* (2018); Emmy, *Zoey's Extraordinary Playlist* (2020)

THE DANCERS

Fourteen backup dancers supported Swift onstage. Some were experienced and had already toured with big-name artists. Others had years of dance experience but had never gone on tour before.

TAYLOR BANKS

- **Notable Work:** *Dancing with the Stars, The Voice, Good Morning America*
- **Notable Artists Worked With:** Cher, Justin Timberlake, Dua Lipa, Billie Eilish

AUDREY DOUGLASS

- **Notable Work:** *Glee,* The Grammys*, America's Got Talent, La La Land*
- **Notable Artists Worked With:** Dua Lipa, Gwen Stefani, Beyoncé, Kesha, The Weeknd

KAREN CHUANG

- **Notable Work:** *Come Dance with Me, Step Into . . . The Movies, Glee, Grease Live!*
- **Notable Artists Worked With:** Kanye West, Lady Gaga, Janet Jackson, P!NK, Nicki Minaj, Khalid

TORI EVANS

- **Notable Work:** *Jimmy Kimmel Live!, The Masked Singer, The Kelly Clarkson Show*
- **Notable Artists Worked With:** Ricky Martin, Maroon 5, Tyga, Cardi B, Jennifer Hudson

TAMIYA LEWIS
- **Notable Work:** MVA pro dancer with Velocity Dance Convention

SAM MCWILLIAMS
- **Notable Work:** *So You Think You Can Dance*
- **Notable Artists Worked With:** Bebe Rexha, Meghan Trainor

SYDNEY MOSS
- **Notable Work:** *Billboard Music Awards, Crazy Ex-Girlfriend, Dolly Parton's Mountain Magic Christmas*
- **Notable Artists Worked With:** Doja Cat, Justin Timberlake, Jennifer Lopez

Swift's backup dancers help set the tone of each Era.

THE ERAS TOUR

NATALIE PETERSON

- **Notable Work:** Embassy Ball World Champion, Karol G's Bichota Tour, *Billboard* Music Awards

JAN RAVNIK

- **Notable Work:** awarded Best Dancer in Slovenia twice, *Billboard* Music Awards, *Dick Clark's New Year's Rockin' Eve*
- **Notable Artists Worked With:** Lewis Capaldi, Bruno Mars, Paula Abdul, Khalid

NATALIE REID

- **Notable Work:** *Are You There God? It's Me, Margaret*, *America's Got Talent*, Tony Awards, *Saturday Night Live*
- **Notable Artists Worked With:** Kacey Musgraves, Adele, Pitbull, Flo Rida, Christina Aguilera

KAMERON SAUNDERS

- **Notable Work:** *The Color Purple*, *Spirited*

> The backup dancers needed to have dancing and acting skills as well as vocal talents.

Swift's dancers came from a variety of backgrounds and experiences.

KEVIN SCHEITZBACH

- **Notable Work:** White Party with Paula Abdul, Coachella with 88Rising, Disney's *Zombies 2*
- **Notable Artists Worked With:** Paula Abdul, Imagine Dragons, Meghan Trainor

RAPHAEL THOMAS

- **Notable Artists Worked With:** Mary J. Blige, John Legend, Janet Jackson

WHYLEY YOSHIMURA

- **Notable Work:** Janet Jackson's Unbreakable World Tour, Rihanna's Last Girl on Earth tour
- **Notable Artists Worked With:** Jennifer Lopez, Justin Bieber

THE MUSICIANS

Backup vocalists sing and dance with the main artist onstage. Their voices provide harmony with the main song, giving a richer sound. Swift has a group of four backup singers she brings on tour. They call themselves The Starlights. They first performed with Swift at the 2012 *MTV Video Music Awards*, backing Swift up on "We Are Never Ever Getting Back Together." They also toured with Swift during her *Red*, *1989*, and *Reputation* tours.

THE STARLIGHTS:

- **Jeslyn Gorman**
- **Kamilah Marshall**
- **Melanie Nyema**
- **Eliotte Nicole Woodford**

The Starlights have their own choreography.

Swift's backup band is called The Agency. They have played with her since Swift's 2008 music video for "Picture to Burn." They got their name from the matching suits, Chuck Taylor shoes, and glasses they wore in the video that made them look like secret agents.

Amos Heller (far left), Michael Meadows (far right) and Paul Sidoti (not pictured) have been with The Agency since Taylor's *Fearless* days.

THE AGENCY:

- **David Cook:** Piano, keyboards
- **Max Bernstein:** Guitar, keyboards
- **Matt Billingslea:** Drums
- **Paul Sidoti:** Guitar
- **Amos Heller:** Bass
- **Mike Meadows:** Guitar, keyboards, vocals
- **Karina DePiano:** Keyboards

THE STAGE

THE MAIN STAGE

The main stage is made of three separate stages connected by a ramp. A huge, curved screen, made of LED panels, arches across the back. It gives even the farthest-away fans an up-close view of Swift. CO2 Jets along the edges of each stage shoot plumes into the air to emphasize key notes or moments in songs.

A long, rectangular runway stage is set perpendicular to the main stage, creating a *T* shape. A small stage is at the far end. During one song, a hole opens up here and Swift dives into it.

In the center of the long stage is a diamond-shaped middle stage. It is lined by straight and round floor lights. Inside the diamond is a series of risers. A rectangular riser section in the center can lift Swift above the audience. Each section can be raised or lowered to create stages for The Agency, The Starlights, or the dancers.

The stage floor is made up of interactive LED panels. This allows for digital visuals such as Swift "swimming" the length of the stage and cracking the ground with each stomp as she performs "Delicate."

FUN FACT

The main stage was designed to be exactly as wide as a football field. A long runway-shaped stage stretches out through the crowd. This allows Swift to get as close to her audience as possible.

THE STAGE

STAGE 1 **LOVER**

The Eras Tour stage is huge. But it's not just a plain stage. Each Era has its own set, complete with color palette, light themes, set pieces, and backdrops. The show begins in the diamond-shaped center stage, with dancers wearing huge silk fans in shades of pink, purple, and orange. The dancers bend down, and the fans cover the stage. When they stand again, Swift is revealed at their center.

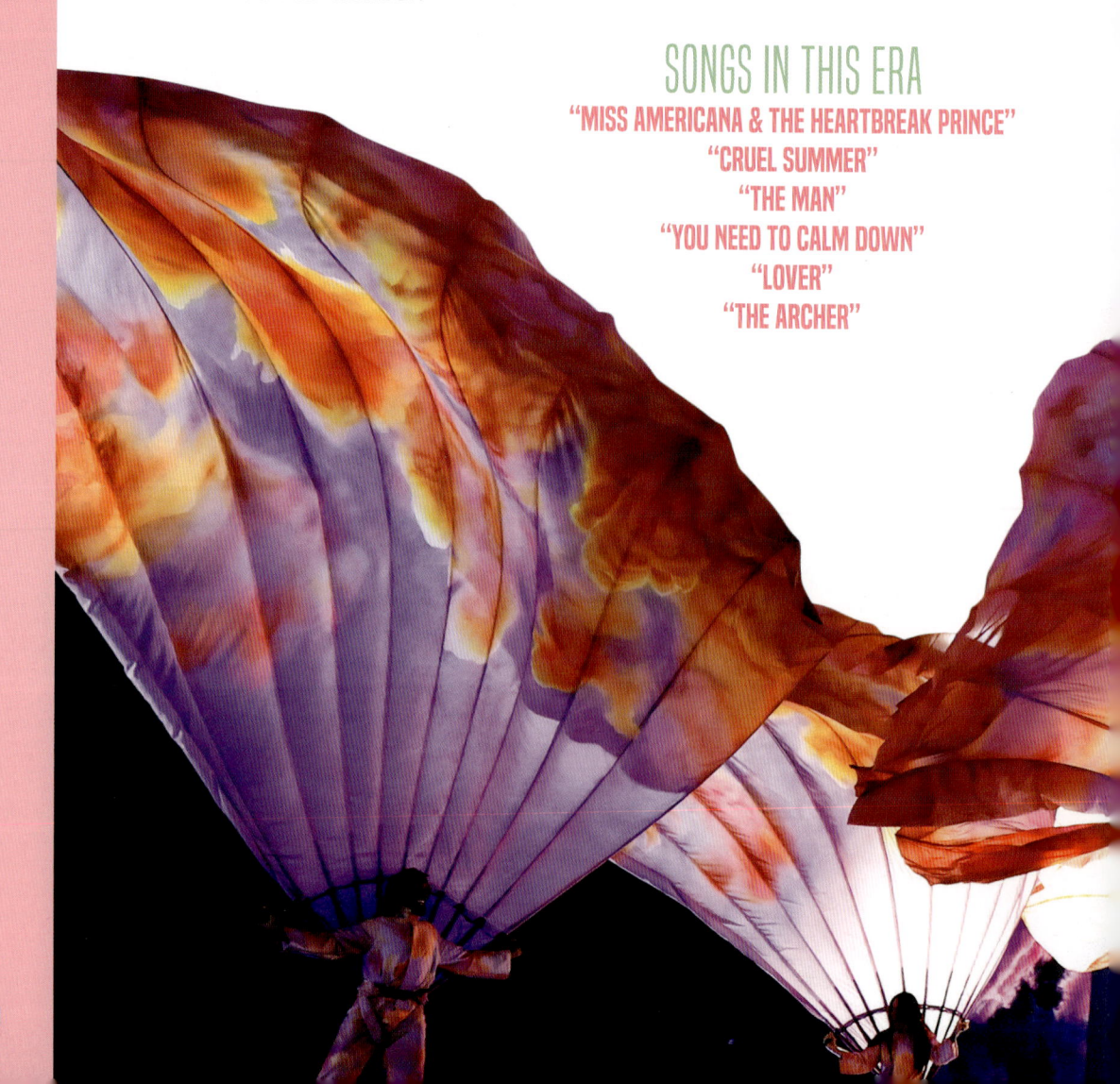

SONGS IN THIS ERA
"MISS AMERICANA & THE HEARTBREAK PRINCE"
"CRUEL SUMMER"
"THE MAN"
"YOU NEED TO CALM DOWN"
"LOVER"
"THE ARCHER"

Romantic fairy-tale scenes are shown on the curved LED screens during "Miss Americana & the Heartbreak Prince" and "Cruel Summer." The arched doorways pull viewers into the singer's dream world.

During "The Man," the main stage is set to resemble a three-tiered office, with workers at desks. The set is black and lined with white lights. The workers wear blacks and grays intended to blend in.

As "The Man" transitions to "You Need to Calm Down," the Lover House appears. The pink "Lover" room is highlighted during its corresponding song.

FUN FACT

The risers are in rectangular layers because the risers themselves are too tall to be stored underneath the stage. Instead, they are stored like steps. As each layer is raised, they are pulled in and popped into place.

STAGE 2 FEARLESS

A curtain of blinding gold rains down from the ceiling, illuminating the otherwise-dark stage. The word FEARLESS appears on the screen. Golds, yellows, and oranges cover the diamond-shaped stage, which, combined with the runway, resembles Swift's silver rhinestone-covered guitar. The stage lights alternate silver and gold.

SONGS IN THIS ERA
"FEARLESS"
"YOU BELONG WITH ME"
"LOVE STORY"

FUN FACT
The microphone changes color with every Era. For some Eras, the mic is covered in matching crystals.

The lifts for the risers never go as high as possible. This keeps Swift and anyone else on the risers safe.

Swift's guitar is a central style theme to the Fearless stage.

    The *Fearless* stage is simple, utilizing the risers during "You Belong With Me," but otherwise allowing Swift to travel the entire stage length to connect with the audience. Fan wristbands alternate between yellow and silver, twinkling like stars. Spotlights send rays of white into the sky. At the end of the song, Swift steps to the center of the diamond-shaped stage and is lowered beneath.

THE LIGHTS ARE SO BRIGHT, BUT THEY NEVER BLIND ME

There are moving headlights spaced around the edge of the stage. They can be pointed in any direction. There are also wash lights in between each headlight and wash bar lights.

STAGE 3 EVERMORE

The *Fearless* stage melts into a forest backlit by blues. Tall pine trees grow out of the stage, adding depth to the forest shown on the screen. Gold lights enhance Swift's dancers, who hold glowing gold and orange orbs. Fog rises from the stage, adding to the mystical feel, and the floor panels below light up under each dancer as they move.

SONGS IN THIS ERA
"'TIS THE D— SEASON"
"WILLOW"
"MARJORIE"
"CHAMPAGNE PROBLEMS"
"TOLERATE IT"

GETTING CREATIVE
Ethan Tobman was the creative director for the Eras Tour. Tobman had worked with Swift during the 2021 Grammy Awards, as well as music videos for "The Man," "Anti-Hero," and "cardigan."

Swift uses her time at the piano to interact with her audience, addressing fan theories and talking about *evermore*.

THE STAGE

During "marjorie," a huge oak tree seems to grow from the stage. After, Swift makes her way to a moss-covered piano that is shaded under a collection of enormous roots illuminated by a single lamp. The scene creates an intimate experience as Swift sings "champagne problems."

A long dining table appears, and Swift sets it with flowers and plates and pours herself a drink. A man comes out to sit at one end of the table. Swift sits at the other end and sings "tolerate it." The back screen is made to look like walls in a huge, empty room, giving the set—and the relationship Swift sings about—a bleak feel.

Fans were enthralled to see life-size trees rise up through the stage floor to give the *evermore* stage an immersive feel.

FUN FACT
Swift played a moss-covered piano in her "cardigan" music video.

STAGE 4 REPUTATION

The set goes black. A spotlight appears. Swift steps into the light. Her every word is emphasized with flashes of long white spotlights. The floors and screens alternate white industrial lines, ladders, and lights with red-and-black snakes. The risers stretch across the center stage, constantly moving and changing their heights.

The aggressive feel of "...Ready For It?" fades out. The dancers fall back, and the lights soften to focus on Swift. Huge cracks created by light begin stretching across the stage as Swift sings "Delicate." As the song hits its peak, Swift leaps into the air and hits the ground causing the entire stage to crack like a windowpane.

Lights along the outside of the center stage shoot in the air like cell bars as Swift transitions to "Don't Blame Me." They grow along the rest of the stage as the song progresses. The LED screens along the riser platforms have candles projected along their fronts.

Bright bars of light surround Swift as she sings.

FUN FACT
The lights from the show were so bright in Tampa, Florida, that people outside Raymond James Stadium thought they were seeing a UFO.

As Swift breaks into "Look What You Made Me Do," dancers pop up along the backstage inside light-edged glass boxes. Similar-shaped boxes move along the stage floor. Each dancer looks like a past version of Swift. Eventually, they break out and surround Swift as she rises above them. The Era closes with a huge snake hissing as Swift passes by.

SONGS IN THIS ERA
"...READY FOR IT?"
"DELICATE"
"DON'T BLAME ME"
"LOOK WHAT YOU MADE ME DO"

The lighted boxes holding past Swifts are inspired by the "Look What You Made Me Do" music video.

THE STAGE

STAGE 5 SPEAK NOW

The reds, blacks, and aggressive industrial lights transition to soft purple. Fog covers the entire backstage floor, creating a lavender glow. The screen behind Swift shows a field of purple that extends to the stage floor. With a huge section of the screen zoomed in on Swift, it creates an illusion, as though Swift is both on the stage and in the field of flowers. The LED wristbands worn by the audience blink pale blue and light purple during the chorus of "Enchanted."

SONGS IN THIS ERA
"ENCHANTED"
"LONG LIVE"

SEPARATE SCREENS

The two screens on either side of the main screen are slightly angled out. There are also smaller screens on either side of the main stage, so people on the sides or slightly behind the stage can see what's going on.

Fans speculated that Swift's *Speak Now* set list was so short because she hadn't yet recorded *(Taylor's Version)* of the album. "Long Live" was added to the tour's set list the same day *Speak Now (Taylor's Version)* was released.

STAGE 6 RED

Red balloons fly out of a red box before Swift appears to sing "22." Her backup dancers surround the red box, which moves across the stage throughout the number. The stage floor flashes red lines, chevrons, and boxes in fun pulses of color. The "22" dancers skip along the backstage for most of the song, letting the runway pop on its own. As the song reaches its peak, they make their way to the center of the stage as confetti flies around them. Eventually, Swift finds herself at the edge of the small stage, where she interacts with a different chosen fan every night.

The dancers skip back to the center stage, where "We Are Never Ever Getting Back Together" begins. The stage floor pulses with spiraling squares, as though driving the point of the song across. The choreography is fun and gossipy.

Although the dancers, set, and costumes don't change for "I Knew You Were Trouble," the entire feeling of the stage does. The back screen shows three close-up views of Swift as she bares all during the confessional. Then, the arena goes dark for "All Too Well (10 Minute Version)."

SONGS IN THIS ERA
"22"
"WE ARE NEVER EVER GETTING BACK TOGETHER"
"I KNEW YOU WERE TROUBLE"
"ALL TOO WELL (10 MINUTE VERSION)"

CO2 Jets emphasize Swift's lyrics, especially during "I Knew You Were Trouble."

STAGE 7 FOLKLORE

The center stage and the back screen rotate with a blue-green forest before settling upright, paving the way for Swift. She sits on top of a moss-covered cabin. Smoke rises from its chimney as the trees on the screen slowly glide in the background, creating the illusion of a moving house.

SONGS IN THIS ERA
"THE 1"
"BETTY"
"THE LAST GREAT AMERICAN DYNASTY"
"AUGUST"
"ILLICIT AFFAIRS"
"MY TEARS RICOCHET"
"CARDIGAN"

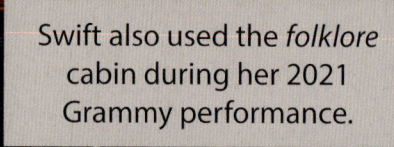

Swift also used the *folklore* cabin during her 2021 Grammy performance.

Some of the beautiful details of the folklore stage are easier to see in the movie than in concert.

Swift introduces the audience to *folklore* from the fantasy cabin, where she performs "the 1" and "betty." The Agency and the backing singers sit on the steps leading up to the cabin. The goal is to make the audience feel like they are watching a group of friends gathered around a campfire.

A blue-and-teal train puffs across the screen behind the cabin before becoming an ocean view. Swift's dancers bring the story of "the last great american dynasty" to life. For a moment, the quaint cottagecore cabin becomes a seaside estate.

Swift leaves the cabin to sing "august." A stormy backdrop sets the mood for Swift's emotional performance of "illicit affairs." Glimmering dresses, images of tears, and blinking white lights appear for "my tears ricochet." The crowd's LED wristbands sparkle as Swift closes the Era with "cardigan."

THE STAGE

STAGE 8 1989

The *1989* Era opens with Swift and her dancers rising up from below the stage. Prerecorded dance moves play on the big screen, working in tandem with the actual dancing. Each dancer has black-and-white outfits from different fashion eras. The lights along the stage floor stretch and cross, shrinking to create the illusion of runways.

During "Blank Space," the center risers lift Swift into the air. Every other block contains a version of Swift in a different outfit. Light-up bikes and golf clubs illuminate the stage.

SONGS IN THIS ERA
"STYLE"
"BLANK SPACE"
"SHAKE IT OFF"
"WILDEST DREAMS"
"BAD BLOOD"

Dancers destroy an interactive image of a car onstage during "Blank Space."

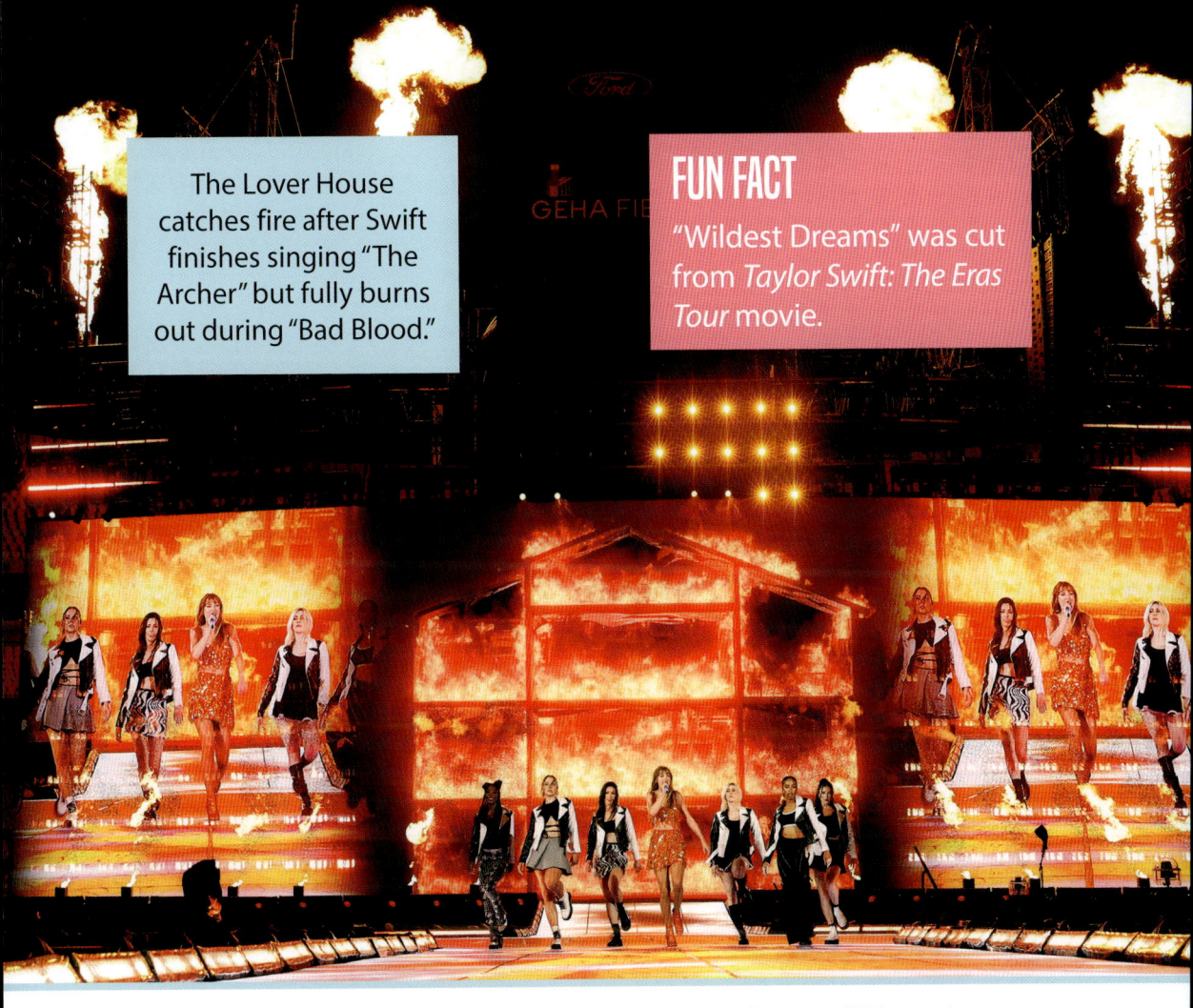

> The Lover House catches fire after Swift finishes singing "The Archer" but fully burns out during "Bad Blood."

> **FUN FACT**
> "Wildest Dreams" was cut from *Taylor Swift: The Eras Tour* movie.

    The set and outfits are the same for "Shake It Off," but the stage lights change the entire vibe. A rotating series of pulsing circles, squares, and lines match the energy of the song. Blue and orange give the song a poppy club feel.

    But then, the stage turns red, square by square. It is time for "Bad Blood." Balls of fire burst across the LED screens, both in the back and on the floor. Red balls of light travel across the audience, floating up and out. On the big screen, Swift strikes a lighter and tosses it into the Lover House. The flames burn blue before turning red and orange, framed by real pyrotechnics.

THE STAGE

STAGE 9 SURPRISE SONGS

Presenting acoustic songs in a football stadium can be a huge challenge. People near the stage have a much different sound and viewing experience than people who have seats hundreds of feet away.

The main sound system is mounted above the main stage. These sets of speakers are called line arrays. Fourteen front-of-house line arrays are enough to cover the sound throughout the stadium. However, there are also speakers on the trees called delays. The delays are precisely timed so the sounds from both sets of speakers reach the audience at the same time.

DEEP DIVE

At the end of her acoustic set, Swift dives below the stage. The stage floor seems to show Swift swimming back to the main stage. A green light tells Swift when it's safe to jump in. Then Swift is carted back so she can start the next set.

The acoustic guitar Swift played is an updated version of the one she used as a teenager.

> The flowers that adorn the Surprise Song piano marry beautifully with Taylor's dresses.

    The spotlights used on the Eras Tour serve as both lights and speakers. They also have cameras, which allow unique views. The spotlights are on tall metal trees, which are placed away from the stage. The lights can wash the stage with different colors or create a spotlight on Swift or others on stage. There are also wash lights pointed toward the audience, making people feel like they're part of the show. Each of the four trees holds two spotlights. There are also two spotlights mounted above the LED screen.

STAGE 10 MIDNIGHTS

Swift begins *Midnights* by climbing up a ladder and into a cloud on the main stage. Each of her dancers come onstage wheeling cotton candy clouds atop ladders, where they meet Swift coming out of the center stage once again. The stage floor and the big screen are covered in images of fluffy purple clouds. The audience's wristbands turn violet to make the stadium look like a beautiful sky of purple.

Then the purple is gone and "Anti-Hero" begins. Swift is momentarily alone on the stage, left to her own devices. The big screen shows an enormous Swift towering over a city skyline, knocking over buildings with every step.

The risers become a staircase and the screens become a shower of midnight rain as the next song begins. Spotlights gather in staggered arrays like bouquets, creating a rainy haze along the edge and rear of the stage. Backup dancers holding

SONGS IN THIS ERA
"LAVENDER HAZE"
"ANTI-HERO"
"MIDNIGHT RAIN"
"VIGILANTE S—"
"BEJEWELED"
"MASTERMIND"
"KARMA"

Dancers move large purple clouds around the stage during "Lavender Haze."

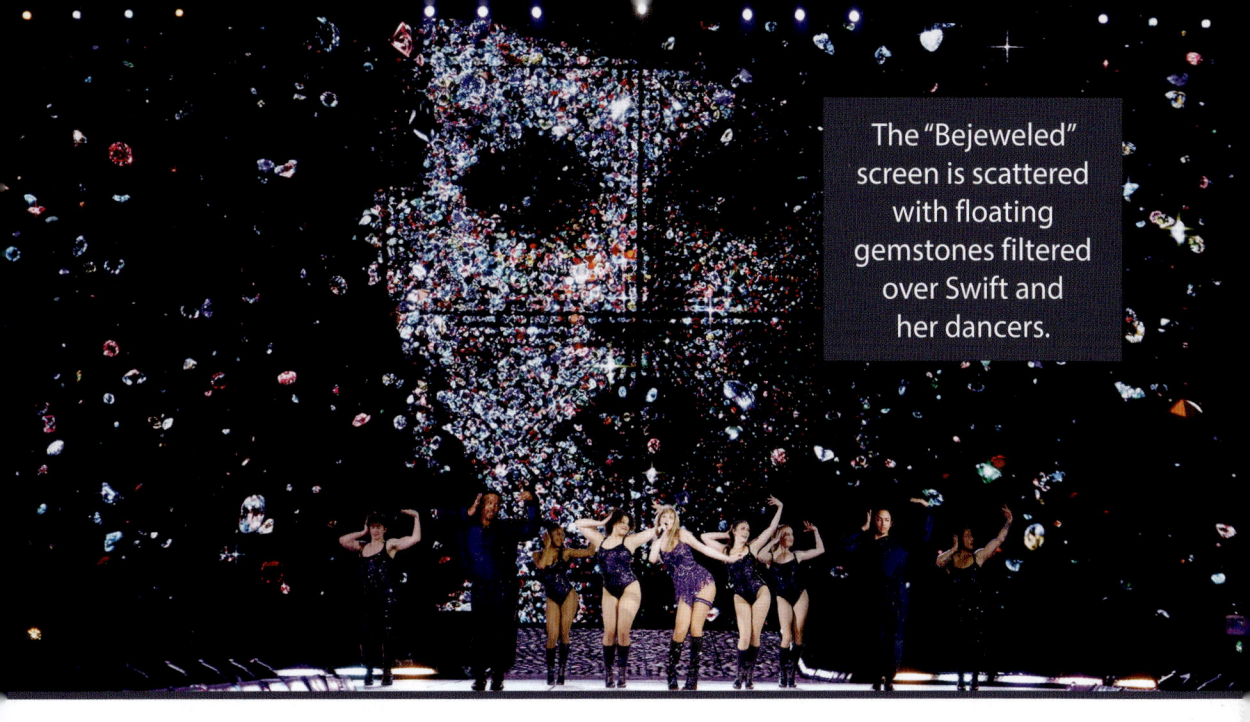

The "Bejeweled" screen is scattered with floating gemstones filtered over Swift and her dancers.

umbrellas huddle together, then break away, revealing that Swift has made a costume change.

The middle stage opens, revealing Swift's backup dancers cast in shadows. Each sits on a chair, individually spotlighted. Then they are lifted in staggered layers on the risers, with Swift at its center. As the show transitions from "Vigilante S—" to "Bejeweled," jewels rain down from the big screen as light facets and rhinestones shine off the stage floor. The stage is accented with amethyst, sapphire, and citron.

The stage turns into a checkerboard for "Mastermind." Flashing lights add to the building drama as Swift's backup performers come onstage dressed in black sequins. Finally, it is time for "Karma." An orange door lowers from the ceiling. The stage gives viewers touches of color representing the Eras that had come before. Confetti rains down, covering the crowd. The far edge of the runway turns orange as Swift's dancers and musicians dance off. The stage opens, swallowing Swift. Fireworks erupt. It is the end of the show.

THE COSTUMES

LOVER

Swift had more than 40 different outfits she wore throughout the tour. Not every outfit was worn on the same night—many had different colorways or slight variations or combinations. But each Era had its own special look, and each look was custom-made to fit that Era's vibe.

The Eras Tour opened with Swift in an Atelier Versace bodysuit. The first of these bodysuits was pink and blue, to match the look of the album art as well as the set design. She paired it with knee-high Eleonora Botta boots made by Christian Louboutin. Thousands of crystals cover the boots, and the red outsole pops onstage.

Fans were surprised to see a second version of the bodysuit as well. Instead of pink and blue, Swift was covered in blue and gold. Her necklace and boots followed this colorway as well.

Swift flexes her muscles as her set transitions from "Cruel Summer" to "The Man."

FUN FACT

Swift's microphone is bejeweled to coordinate with the pink-and-blue bodysuit.

Swift added a matching floral necklace, also by Versace, to later shows.

THE COSTUMES

Swift's all-pink *Lover* bodysuit is paired with bubblegum pink Christian Louboutin boots.

In New Jersey, Swift pulled out a purple version of the Atelier Versace bodysuit. This time, it was purple and gold. Beaded fringe decorated the bottom, and her necklace had butterflies instead of flowers. The boots were purple with an ombre fade to rose gold.

In Buenos Aires, Argentina, Swift showed off an all-pink version of the boots and suit. It did not have fringe, and she donned a crystal choker studded with pink stones.

The bodysuits are covered in crystals and paillettes, a special piece of glittering material. They are similar to sequins. However, sequins have a hole in the center and are meant to sparkle. Paillettes have holes near the edges and are meant to move.

Each bodysuit has subtle differences.

ATELIER VERSACE

Atelier Versace is part of the Versace design label. It makes haute couture pieces, which are exclusive and custom-made. *Atelier* means "workshop" or "studio" in French. Donatella Versace is the sister of company founder Gianni Versace. She became the company's creative director in 1997.

THE COSTUMES

For "The Man," Swift added a Versace blazer over the *Lover* bodysuit. She had three different versions. Each was double-breasted and had Versace's signature Medusa buttons. The blazer she wears with the pink-and-blue bodysuit is silver and matches the silver Christian Louboutin boots.

The second blazer is black with gold pinstripes. She pairs it with the blue-and-gold bodysuit.

JOSEPH CASSELL FALCONER

Swift's personal stylist is Joseph Cassell Falconer. He has been part of her team since *Speak Now*, and Swift is his primary client. Falconer has also styled fashion shoots, music videos, and award show looks.

The first blazer featured on the Eras Tour was silver.

Swift's backup dancers play the role of office workers during "The Man."

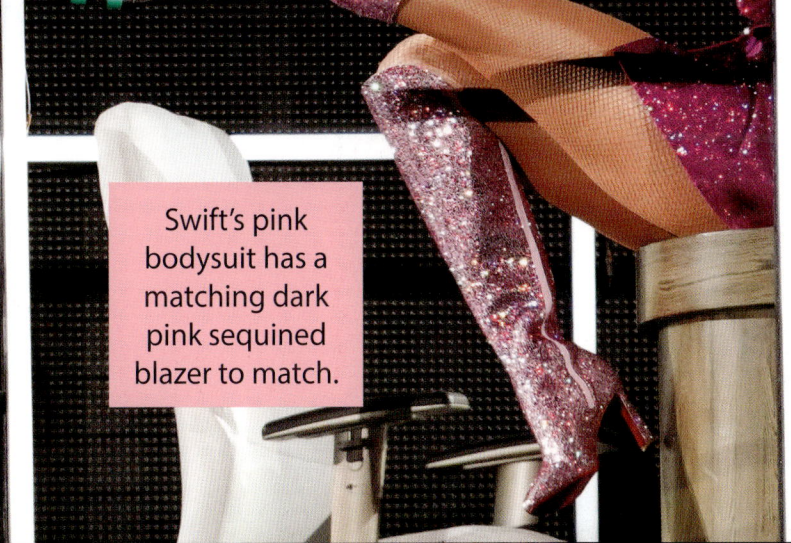

Swift's pink bodysuit has a matching dark pink sequined blazer to match.

FEARLESS

Roberto Cavalli's creative director Fausto Puglisi designed Swift's gold fringed dress for the *Fearless* set. Swift wore a similar dress from the same label during her Speak Now World Tour. The layered zigzag fringe is reminiscent of 1920s flapper fashion.

Swift's dress catches every twist, wiggle, and bump as she moves around the stage.

LUXURY FASHION HOUSE

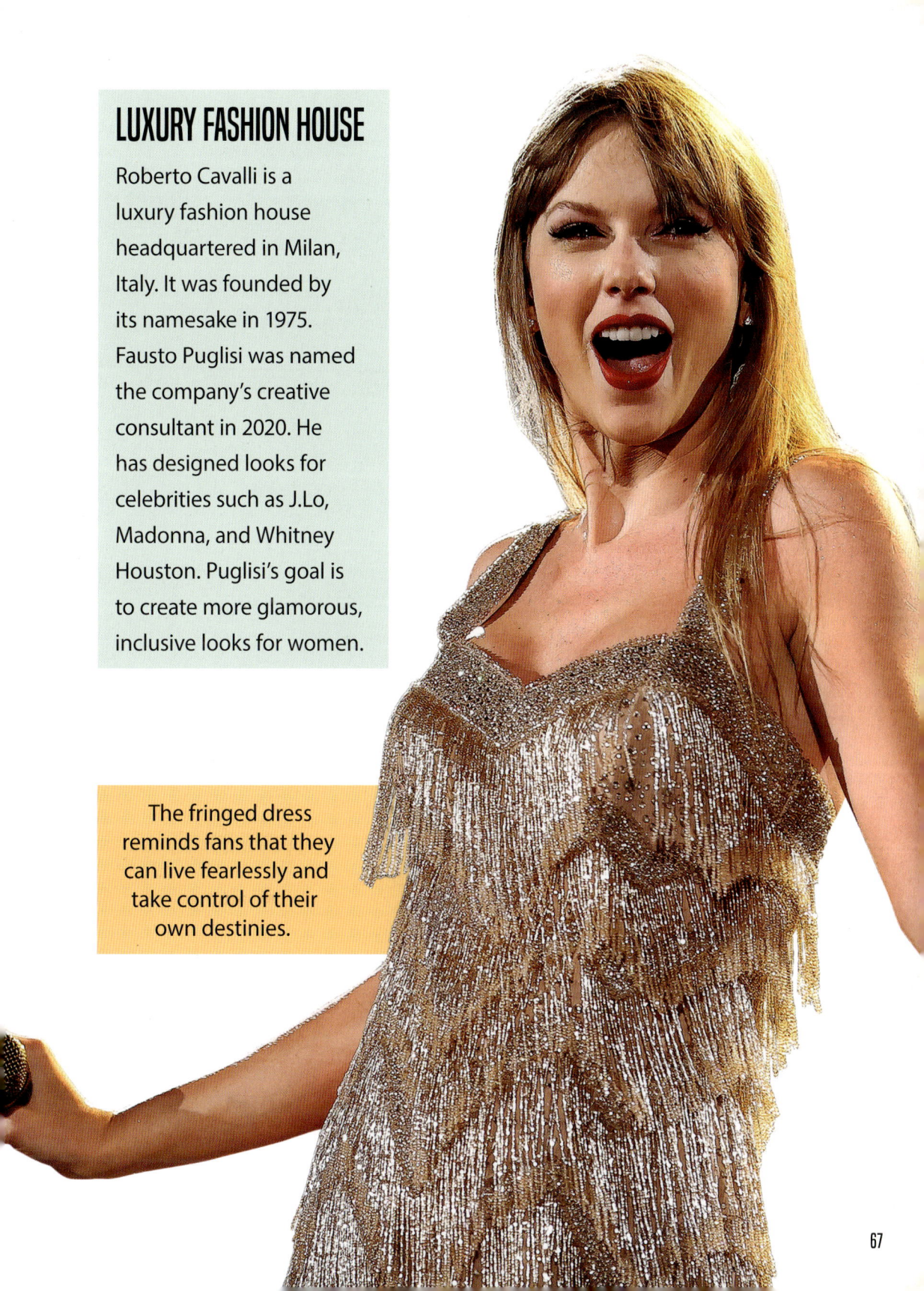

Roberto Cavalli is a luxury fashion house headquartered in Milan, Italy. It was founded by its namesake in 1975. Fausto Puglisi was named the company's creative consultant in 2020. He has designed looks for celebrities such as J.Lo, Madonna, and Whitney Houston. Puglisi's goal is to create more glamorous, inclusive looks for women.

The fringed dress reminds fans that they can live fearlessly and take control of their own destinies.

THE COSTUMES

Roberto Cavalli also created a minidress with longer fringe. It was gold on top and mixed with silver for an ombre effect, fading like a sunset from darkest to lightest. The Swarovski crystals were applied by hand. Swift's boots were made by Christian Louboutin. The Cate boots, not as high as the over-the-knee Eleonora Bottas, were covered in silver crystals.

The Fearless dress sparkles in the light.

PLAY ON

During "Fearless," Swift uses a silver acoustic guitar as a nod to the one she played during her 2009 *Fearless* tour. Swift's parents decorated it themselves, incorporating her lucky number 13 into the design.

EVERMORE

The feel of *evermore* is Bohemian cottagecore, and the Etro dress Swift wore during the set fits that feel. The tie-front dress had ruffled edges, a corset top, and beaded detail. The marigold color coordinated with the moss-colored piano Swift played. Its color calls back to the plaid jacket Swift wears on the cover of the *evermore* album. Even the gold-leaf pattern of the Etro dress reminds fans of the album cover, mimicking Swift's braided hair.

During "willow," Swift wears a green velvet cape over the dress, also designed by Etro. She wears a similar cape during the "willow" music video.

Not even weather could stop the Eras Tour. The show in Foxborough, Massachusetts, went on during a rainstorm.

Swift wears heeled boots under her *evermore* dress.

AN IMMERSIVE EXPERIENCE

During the Eras Tour, everyone in attendance got an LED wristband. The wristbands were synced up to the music using radio waves, infrared technology, and Bluetooth. Lighting operators could use the bracelets to create elaborate patterns, words, or color effects throughout the audience. They helped everyone in attendance feel more connected.

THE COSTUMES

An alternate look Swift wears during *evermore* was designed by Etro creative director Marco De Vincenzo. His contribution is a full burgundy dress made with fil coupé fabric. This type of fabric is embellished with a special technique where threads are woven in an intricate pattern. The dress had ruffled layers and an empire waist.

ETRO

Etro is an Italian fashion design label. Its signature look is paisley prints. The designers also play with global looks such as caftans, kimonos, and vintage hippie looks from the 1960s.

The crowd's LED lights create the illusion of a starry night.

REPUTATION

During Swift's Reputation Stadium Tour in 2018, many of her looks were black bodysuits covered in scalelike sequins. The asymmetrical catsuit worn during her Eras Tour *Reputation* set was reminiscent of that. The Roberto Cavalli one-legged jumpsuit was black but overlaid with red three-dimensional snakes. The suit's right sleeve was mesh, with the snakes covering the right leg, leaving the left arm and leg free.

The dark, intense bodysuit matches *Reputation's* mood and emphasizes the major shift from the *evermore* Era.

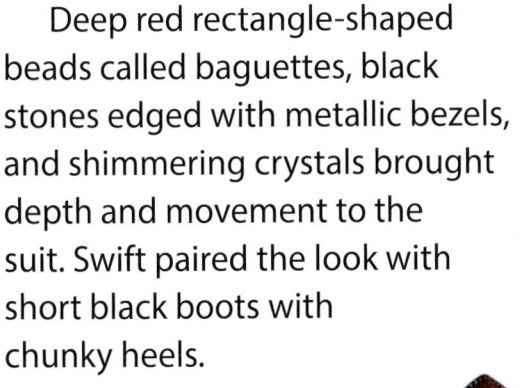

Deep red rectangle-shaped beads called baguettes, black stones edged with metallic bezels, and shimmering crystals brought depth and movement to the suit. Swift paired the look with short black boots with chunky heels.

The snake wrapped around Swift's microphone is an exciting detail that brought fans back to her Reputation Tour.

FUN FACT

Some fans theorized that Swift's *Reputation* Era costume symbolizes her two separate selves. The bodysuit covers half of her body and exposes the other half. One side represents her public persona and the other represents her true, bare self.

SPEAK NOW

The *Speak Now* Era gets the least amount of time on stage, but Swift wore several different dresses to represent it while on tour. During the original *Speak Now* Era from 2010 to 2011, Swift's signature look was princess ball gowns.

The first dress Swift wore was a pale pink tulle-skirted ball gown designed by Nicole + Felicia. The skirt is embroidered with gold sparkles reminiscent of the purple flowers splashed across the huge screen behind Swift as she sings.

NICOLE + FELICIA

Nicole + Felicia are sisters based in Taiwan. They opened a couture brand in 2015. Initially, their brand was focused on brides, but they also specialize in evening wear and bespoke looks. They worked closely with Swift's stylist, Joseph Cassell Falconer. Nicole + Felicia also designed the wedding dress Swift wore in her "I Bet You Think About Me" music video.

The first time dress designer Nicole Chang saw Swift wearing her creation was on opening night of the tour.

THE COSTUMES

ZUHAIR MURAD

Zuhair Murad is a Lebanese designer now based in Italy. He made his break in 2009 when celebrities first wore his looks on the red carpet. One of his dresses was worn by Saudi Arabian Princess Ameera Al-Taweel to attend Prince William and Kate's Royal Wedding.

Designer Zuhair Murad created a pink princess gown for the *Speak Now* Era. The bodice is tightly beaded in a starburst pattern, with vertical lines of hand-applied sequins creating a rain-like effect. The dress uses 164 feet (50 m) of tulle and took more than 350 hours of labor.

FUN FACT

Tulle is a sheer, netlike fabric made from fine threads. Dressmakers often use it for wedding or formal dresses. It can be layered, and moves naturally.

Zuhair Murad released short videos that gave fans a behind-the-scenes glimpse into each dress's creation.

Swift wears two Elie Saab gowns during *Speak Now*. The first is a couture gown encrusted with beads and accented with floral tulle appliques. It's from the designer's Haute Couture Autumn/Winter 2022-2023 collection. The gown is less full than some of the other princess styles Swift wore, and the top is more fitted, but the look still captures the dreamlike feel of the Era.

ELIE SAAB

Elie Saab is a Lebanese designer who makes evening wear for brides and celebrities. His style combines Middle Eastern embellishments with western silhouettes. He first rose to fame when Halle Berry accepted an Oscar while wearing a dress he made. Since then, he has dressed royalty, movie stars, and other celebrities.

Beads, sequins, and organza flowers cascade down the tulle gown.

THE COSTUMES

HAUTE COUTURE

The French word *couture* means "dressmaking" or "sewing." *Haute* means "high." Fashion designers create haute couture for a specific client or type of client. Then the pieces are created by hand, using expensive, high-quality materials and thousands of hours of labor.

Swift has been wearing Elie Saab styles since 2011.

The second dress designed by Elie Saab was from the designer's Autumn 2020 Couture collection. Originally, the dress had a short, feathered cape, which Swift opted to remove. The bodice is covered in silver appliques that burst out from its center and cascade over the layered tulle skirt.

The pale dress takes on the hues of the stage and big screen, appearing gold at some angles and lilac in others.

THE COSTUMES

The lilac dress is made of 1,500 feet (457 m) of tulle and 3,000 crystals.

Nicole + Felicia designed two more gowns for *Speak Now*. The first is a layered dress in ombre shades ranging from pale purple to deep lavender. The colors match the flower field in the set's background and are a tribute to *Speak Now*'s color palette.

The third Nicole + Felicia dress Swift wore was light blue. It was fully beaded and took 2,100 hours to make. Swift wore it on August 9, 2023, to celebrate the upcoming release of *1989 (Taylor's Version)*.

FUN FACT

Nicole + Felicia also designed matching gold-and-purple gowns for Swift's backup dancers.

THE COSTUMES

RED

In the 2013 "22" music video, Swift wears a T-shirt that says, "Not a lot going on at the moment." That shirt was designed by Ashish Gupta and was paired with shorts and a black fedora.

For Swift's *Red* Era, Gupta came back to recreate—and update—that look. A word has been removed and now the tee reads, "A lot going on at the moment." The words "A lot" were red.

The high shorts have been replaced too. Underneath the tee, Swift wears an ombre bodysuit that is revealed during "I Knew You Were Trouble."

Swift pairs both looks with CL Moc Lug loafers by Christian Louboutin. The loafers have thick rubber soles.

> Swift has more than 40 different outfits. Each of her backup dancers, musicians, and singers have their own outfits for each set too.

FUN FACT
Fans could buy the "22" shirt seen in the music video. It cost $895 and sold out the same day.

THE COSTUMES

The updated "22" shirt wasn't the only tee Swift wore. One version of the same style said, "Who's Taylor Swift anyway? Ew." The word *ew* was red. Another said, "We are never getting back together. Like ever." The words *never* and *ever* were red, while the rest of the text was black.

During every performance of "We Are Never Ever Getting Back Together," Swift hands backup dancer Kameron Saunders (left) the microphone for a quote.

FUN FACT

The black fedora hat was designed by Gladys Tamez. She has designed hats for celebrities such as Lil Nas X, LeBron James, Lady Gaga, and Billy Ray Cyrus.

Fans began to wonder if Swift was showing them a secret message. The red letters were all found in *Speak Now (Taylor's Version)*. Swift had hidden similar hints to announce the Speak Now World Tour. Their theories were validated on May 5, 2023, when Swift announced that the rerecorded *Speak Now* album would be out later that year.

THE COSTUMES

Fans are divided over Swift's ombre bodysuit and jacket. Some say it is boring. Others say it is classic.

Swift shed the tee to reveal the black-and-red ombre bodysuit underneath. The *Red* bodysuit is another piece designed by Ashish Gupta.

ASHISH GUPTA

Ashish Gupta is an Indian fashion designer based in London. Hand-embroidered sequins, bold slogans, and nightlife outfits are part of his signature look. Creating collections that push equality and inclusivity are part of his brand's commitment.

Swift added a long duster jacket with a pointed collar, also designed by Gupta, for "All Too Well (10 Minute Version)." The ombre effect is repeated along the length of the duster. The guitar Swift played was either a rich maroon or bedazzled in black rhinestones outlined in white.

Even the microphone stand matches the look.

THE COSTUMES

> **FUN FACT**
> Swift wears ballet flats during the *folklore* set.

FOLKLORE

folklore took fans back to a dreamy world, and Swift's outfits changed the mood to match. The lilac Alberta Ferretti gown was flowy, with long sleeves and a layered skirt. Chiffon flowed as Swift turned in place, draping delicately when she was at rest. The sleeves and layered skirts were tapered to a *V* shape and accented with lace.

> **ALBERTA FERRETTI**
> Alberta Ferretti is an Italian fashion designer. Her style focuses on femininity and romance, creating a delicate profile. Ferretti opened her own boutique at the age of 18 and has since made a name for herself in fashion.

> A dark stripe near the bottom of the dress's hem is covered with embroidery and beads.

THE COSTUMES

    The creamy off-white Alberta Ferretti dress had shorter sleeves, with a cape-like addition that billowed around Swift's shoulders. Gold feathers were embroidered on the bodice and over the shoulder caps, and clear crystals picked up every hint of light. The skirt was layered with three graduating tiers of fabric. More subtle feathering on the skirt and sleeves resembled the tall pine trees in the set's background. They were much more subtle but could be seen when Swift moved freely.

The Ferretti dresses seems to float when Swift spins—which she does every night!

> Flutter sleeves can be used like a cape or tossed off the shoulder like wings.

THE COSTUMES

> The lightweight chiffon moves with Swift's body, swinging and floating to create drama.

Alberta Ferretti's green leaf dress is more revealing than the others. Leaves are embroidered over the bodice, which has a more plunging neckline and reveals a hint of skin through a thin layer of mesh.

Swift also wore a pink version of this dress. Instead of subtle gold, the entire front of the pink dress was embroidered, with sequin accents for a sparkle.

> Ferretti's green dress looks like different shades of green depending on how the light hits it.

THE COSTUMES

Swift wore a flowing blue Alberta Ferretti dress on August 9, 2023. During this show, she announced that *1989 (Taylor's Version)* was on its way.

Each of the Ferretti dresses were similar but had their own subtle, special elements to help them stand apart.

"In isolation my imagination has run wild and this album is the result, a collection of songs and stories that flowed like a stream of consciousness."

—TAYLOR SWIFT ANNOUNCING THE RELEASE OF *FOLKLORE*

The blue dress is similar to Swift's pink *folklore* dress, but its cool palette is different enough to get the audience's attention.

FUN FACT

1989 (Taylor's Version) was announced at the Los Angeles show in August 2023. Swift wore all five of the blue variant outfits she had.

THE COSTUMES

1989

Swift opened the *1989* act wearing a two-piece set similar to the one she wore during that album's tour. The outfit came in multiple colorways. Designed by Fausto Puglisi for Roberto Cavalli, each outfit was covered in Swarovski crystals, sequins, and silver beads that had been added by hand. Both the bodice and the skirt have a diamond-cross pattern. Beaded fringe dangles from both pieces.

The matching boots Swift wore with each top and skirt were custom-made by Christian Louboutin.

Swift's *1989* Era was a time of reinvention, living life to the fullest, and freedom.

CHRISTIAN LOUBOUTIN

Christian Louboutin is a French fashion designer. Stiletto shoes with red lacquered outsoles are his brand's signature. The shoes are designed to make women feel empowered and confident.

The backup dancers wear black and white to represent Swift's next album, *Reputation*, which was a response to the media scrutiny she received after *1989*.

THE COSTUMES

> Roberto Cavalli's beaded creations shed Swift's teenage country star look and fully embraced her pop Era.

1989 was an important Era for Swift. It was her transition from country singer to pop star. The Roberto Cavalli sequined tops and skirts she wore symbolized that. The outfits came in four colors—blue, orange, green, and pink.

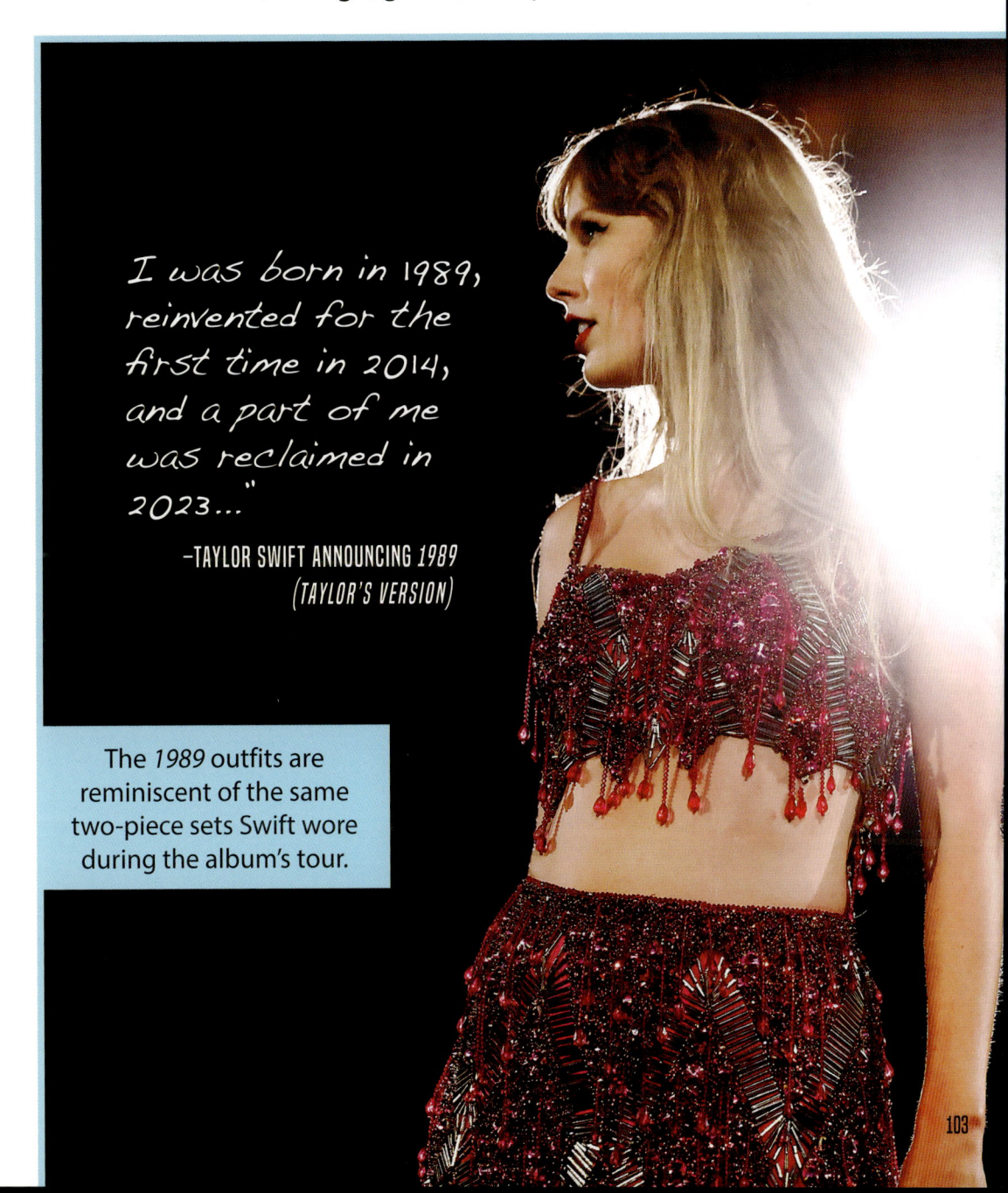

> *I was born in 1989, reinvented for the first time in 2014, and a part of me was reclaimed in 2023..."*
>
> —TAYLOR SWIFT ANNOUNCING *1989 (TAYLOR'S VERSION)*

The *1989* outfits are reminiscent of the same two-piece sets Swift wore during the album's tour.

THE COSTUMES

SURPRISE SONGS

Swift returned to folksy flowing dresses for her acoustic set. Jessica Jones was the mind behind many of Swift's past looks, especially from the *Reputation* Era. For Swift's first surprise acoustic set, she wore a dark pink pleated dress with cap sleeves and layered ruffles down the front. Tiny crystals enhanced the lines of the pleats. A beaded belt wrapped around the waist of the dress to keep it closed.

Swift returns to her country roots by playing a Taylor guitar, the same brand she played as a teenager.

Jessica Jones also dressed Swift for the *1989* and *Reputation* tours.

JESSICA JONES

Jessica Jones is a design professional. She has dressed runway models and red carpet celebrities including Selena Gomez and Camila Cabello. Swift wore a gold Jessica Jones bodysuit and gown at the 2019 American Music Awards, where she won *Billboard* magazine's Woman of the Decade award.

THE COSTUMES

> The acoustic set dress opens just enough to give a peek of the beaded outfit underneath.

The Jessica Jones dresses come in four colors: lush reddish pink, forest green, bright yellow, and sea blue. Each dress goes with the two-piece Roberto Cavalli outfit it matches—pink and pink, orange and yellow, green and green, and blue and blue. The ruffled dress lays over the two-piece set seamlessly for an easy costume change.

Swift announced *1989 (Taylor's Version)* before singing "New Romantics" in Los Angeles.

MIDNIGHTS

Swift begins her *Midnights* Era by climbing out of bed and into a cloud. A crystal T-shirt dress is paired with a lavender faux fur coat. Crystal droplets hang from the coat's fur. The jacket is similar to the one Swift wore in her "Lavender Haze" music video. The jacket comes off during "Anti-Hero," giving the crowd an up-close look at the T-shirt dress, shimmering with pinks, blues, and purples.

> Fans at every stop guess which "Anti-Hero" shirt dress Swift will wear—and if they will see a new color for the very first time.

THE COSTUMES

Swift's footwear for *Midnights* was knee-high Christian Louboutin Gael boots, covered in brilliant glass strass rhinestones.

Like many of her other outfits, Swift has different color variations she switches between, ranging from a blend of pink, purple, and blue to sky blue, dark purple, pink, and light violet.

OSCAR DE LA RENTA

Oscar de la Renta was a Dominican-born American fashion designer. He dressed socialites, movie stars, and political leaders. His label has long been associated with high society. Fernando Garcia was named co-creative director of the fashion label in 2016. He worked on Swift's *Midnights* bodysuit.

THE COSTUMES

> It took 315 hours of labor to create Swift's Oscar de la Renta *Midnights* bodysuit.

Under the sparkling tee is the bodysuit Swift wears to close out the show. The main outfit was a midnight-blue beaded suit by Oscar de la Renta. The fabric was covered in beaded fringe. It was created with more than 5,300 hand-embroidered crystals and beads in shades of deep midnight, blue, and iridescence.

FUN FACT

Zuhair Murad's first *Midnights* bodysuit is adorned with 20,000 sequins and crystals. It took more than 350 hours to complete. A label is sewn inside that says, "For Taylor Swift."

The bodysuit designed by Zuhair Murad adds to the glistening water effect during "Midnight Rain."

THE COSTUMES

Everything about Swift's *Midnights* Era looks scream "Bejeweled."

During her Las Vegas shows, Swift revealed a second *Midnights* outfit. This one was created by Zuhair Murad. It was a similar look to the Oscar de la Renta piece, but the beaded skirt was fuller and the blues were not as dark. It was worn with a matching beaded garter. Twenty thousand hand-sewn sequins and crystals were used to create it.

Another Zuhair Murad bodysuit was revealed during the Los Angeles shows. It was the same deep midnight blue as the Oscar de la Renta outfit. The skirt was also beaded, but less full. The matching beaded garter was more elaborate. The cascading beaded bodice showed hints of skin through mesh layers.

The look of both of Murad's *Midnights* bodysuits mimics the silver couture gown Swift wore in her "Midnights" music video.

THE COSTUMES

> Tinsel played a big role in runway fashion in 2023. Swift's tinsel jackets made the haute couture look even more popular.

"Karma" added a rainbow of color to the stage. The tinsel-covered jackets are worn by everyone, layering shimmering rows of color across the stage. Swift has worn the jacket in multiple colors, including dark pink, midnight blue, multicolor, and bubblegum pink.

> The "Karma" jackets catch the light, adding to the feeling of celebration as the Eras Tour concludes.

THE SET LIST

LOVER

Lover was first released in 2019. It was Swift's seventh studio album. The main theme was love and romance, with songs about happiness but also sadness and mourning. Swift took listeners on a journey through her youth, with high-school-aged Swift blossoming into an adult at the end of her 20s. It was a compilation of everything she had learned, both musically, lyrically, and personally.

Swift said of *Lover*, "This album is really a love letter to love."

ALBUM NOTES

18 tracks
Original release date: August 23, 2019
Writers: Taylor Swift, Jack Antonoff, Adam Feeney, Louis Bell, Cautious Clay, Mark Anthony Spears, Brendon Urie, Annie Clark
Producers: Taylor Swift, Jack Antonoff, Frank Dukes, Louis Bell, Sounwave, Joel Little
Guests: Brendon Urie, The Chicks

ALBUM TRACK LIST

1. "I Forgot That You Existed"
2. "Cruel Summer"
3. "Lover"
4. "The Man"
5. "The Archer"
6. "I Think He Knows"
7. "Miss Americana & the Heartbreak Prince"
8. "Paper Rings"
9. "Cornelia Street"
10. "Death By a Thousand Cuts"
11. "London Boy"
12. "Soon You'll Get Better" (feat. The Chicks)
13. "False God"
14. "You Need to Calm Down"
15. "Afterglow"
16. "ME!" (feat. Brendon Urie)
17. "It's Nice to Have a Friend"
18. "Daylight"

WRITERS: SWIFT, LITTLE
PRODUCERS: SWIFT, LITTLE, FEENEY

MISS AMERICANA & THE HEARTBREAK PRINCE

To kick off the show, Swift chose "Miss Americana & the Heartbreak Prince." The song calls back images of high school, with marching bands, homecoming queens, and prom dresses. Lyrics echo words from *Reputation*, *Taylor Swift*, and *Speak Now*. The song alludes to both a troubled love story and Swift's decision to become more engaged with social issues. The repeated lyrics, "It's been a long time coming," before Swift was revealed on stage were a fitting and exciting way to open her first concert in years.

I counted days, I counted miles / To see you there, to see you there / It's been a long time coming, but / It's you and me, that's my whole world

CRUEL SUMMER

"Cruel Summer" outlines a budding and doomed summer relationship full of secrecy and obsession. Swifties have long argued just who the other person in the relationship might be—since Swift has a history of writing songs about people she's dated.

WRITERS: SWIFT, ANTONOFF, CLARK
PRODUCERS: SWIFT, ANTONOFF

And I screamed for whatever it's worth / "I love you," ain't that the worst thing you ever heard?

SUMMER TOUR

"Cruel Summer" wasn't released as a single until 2023, when Swift started performing it on tour. Even though *Lover* had been out for nearly four years, the song jumped to the top of the Billboard Hot 100 chart.

WRITERS: SWIFT, LITTLE
PRODUCERS: SWIFT, LITTLE

THE SET LIST

THE MAN

"The Man" calls attention to the way society views men and women in the same roles. Swift points out that men are held to a different standard than women and are granted more power based solely on their gender. Things such as serial dating, bragging about money, and being bossy are often applauded when men do them. Yet women who act similarly are judged negatively. Women are often expected to be polite and quiet, and are not believed when they speak up about mistreatment by men. Swift uses her lyrics to wonder how her career might have looked if she were a man.

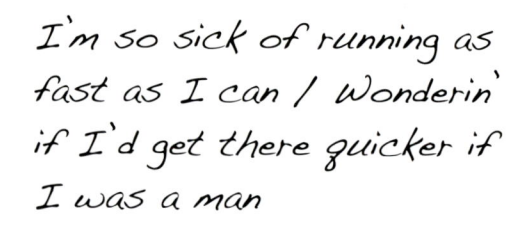

I'm so sick of running as fast as I can / Wonderin' if I'd get there quicker if I was a man

LET THE PLAYERS PLAY

In the music video for "The Man," one scene shows a wall graffitied with names of Swift's earlier albums she recorded with Big Machine Records. There are also two signs. One says "Missing: If Found Return to Taylor Swift." The other is a No Scooters sign. In 2019, Scooter Braun purchased the rights to Swift's music catalog and then prevented her from performing her songs on television. This ushered in the (Taylor's Version) Era.

WRITERS: SWIFT, LITTLE
PRODUCERS: SWIFT, LITTLE

YOU NEED TO CALM DOWN

"You Need to Calm Down" is the second single off *Lover*. Right away, fans compared it to "Mean" from *Speak Now*. Both are about supporting marginalized groups and not letting negativity bring you down. Since her debut as a musician, Swift has dealt with petty bullying and trolling. "You Need to Calm Down" is a message to be brave and not to let what someone else thinks—especially someone on the Internet—control you.

I've learned a lesson that stressin' and obsessin' 'bout somebody else is no fun / And snakes and stones never broke my bones

THE SET LIST

WRITER: SWIFT
PRODUCERS: SWIFT, ANTONOFF

LOVING LOVER

"Lover" was nominated for the 2020 Song of the Year at the Grammy Awards. It was Swift's fourth nomination. "Shake It Off," "Blank Space," and "You Belong With Me" had also been nominated. But the personal message of "Lover" gave this nomination a special meaning.

Ladies and gentlemen, will you please stand / With every guitar string scar on my hand / I take this magnetic force of a man to be my lover

LOVER

Taylor Swift is a romantic, and "Lover" showcases everything good and sentimental about being in a contented, happy relationship. The lyrics start with moving in together and ending with marriage. The song was inspired by her long-term boyfriend at the time, Joe Alwyn. Swift has a lot of songs about breakups and disappointments. "Lover" embraces hopefulness among the hurt. She wanted to inspire people to take a traditional relationship and make it their own.

WRITERS: SWIFT, ANTONOFF
PRODUCERS: SWIFT, ANTONOFF

THE ARCHER

"The Archer" explores Swift's awareness of her imperfections, and how she has had to defend herself in past relationships. As a celebrity who is closely followed by the media, every relationship Swift has—whether friends or partners—gets viewed through a microscope at every phase. The lyrics discuss self-doubt, overthinking, and what happens if, and when, heartbreak happens.

FUN FACT

"The Archer" is the fifth track on *Lover*. Swift often saves the fifth track for songs about vulnerability and honesty.

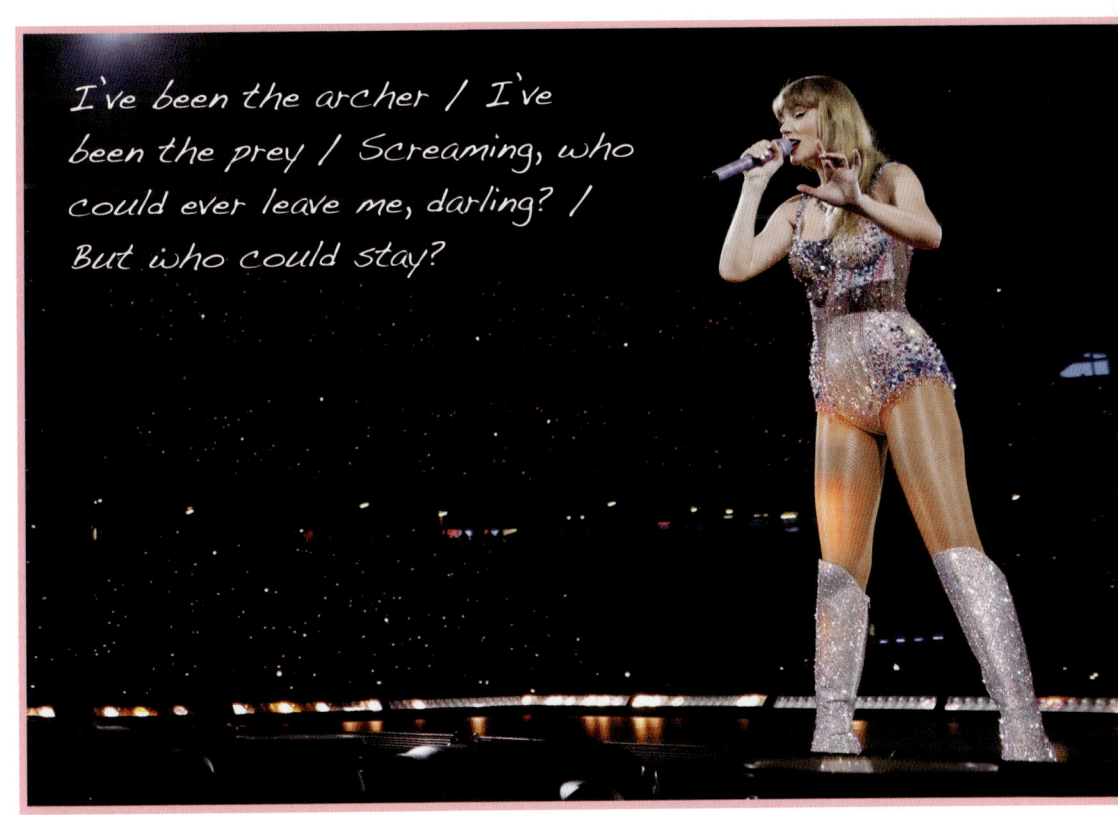

> I've been the archer / I've been the prey / Screaming, who could ever leave me, darling? / But who could stay?

FEARLESS

Fearless is Swift's second album. It has a country-pop-rock sound with acoustic and electric guitars, banjos, fiddles, and mandolins. Following its release, eighteen-year-old Swift became the youngest artist in history to have a best-selling album of the year. *Fearless* spent 11 weeks on Billboard's Top 200, later earning Swift her first Grammy—and her second, third, and fourth. *Fearless* was the album that brought Swift from the country world into the world of chart-topping radio hits.

ALBUM TRACK LIST

1. "Fearless"
2. "Fifteen"
3. "Love Story"
4. "Hey Stephen"
5. "White Horse"
6. "You Belong With Me"
7. "Breathe" (feat. Colbie Caillat)
8. "Tell Me Why"
9. "You're Not Sorry"
10. "The Way I Loved You"
11. "Forever & Always"
12. "The Best Day"
13. "Change"

ALBUM NOTES

13 tracks
Original release date: November 11, 2008
Writers: Taylor Swift, Liz Rose, Hillary Lindsey, Colbie Caillat, John Rich
Producers: Taylor Swift, Nathan Chapman
Guest: Colbie Caillat

FUN FACT

Fearless (Taylor's Version) has 27 tracks. Swift added six unreleased songs from The Vault.

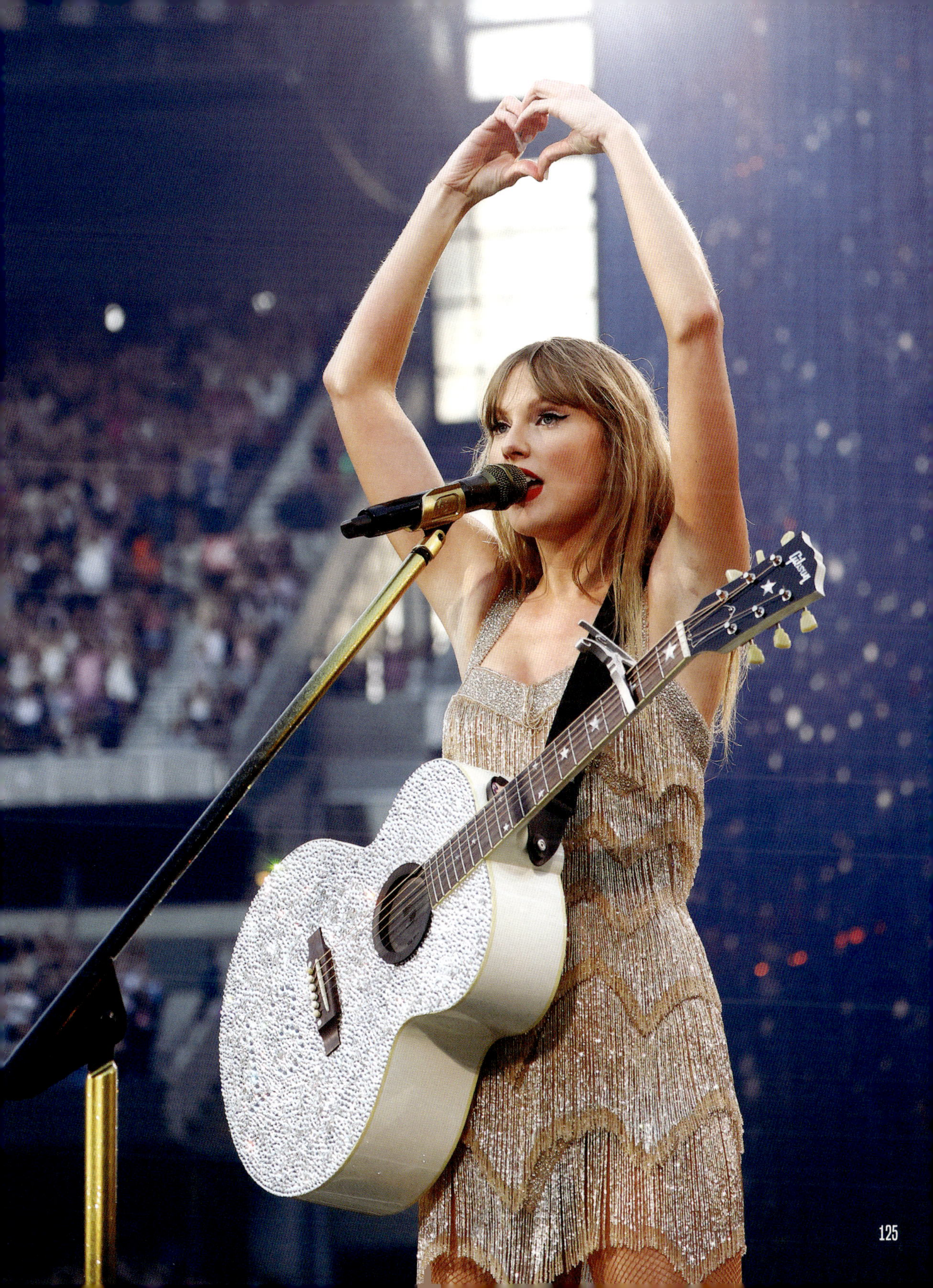

THE SET LIST

WRITERS: SWIFT, ROSE, LINDSEY
PRODUCERS: SWIFT, CHAPMAN

FEARLESS

Swift wrote "Fearless" while touring for her *Taylor Swift* album. She imagined what it might be like to fall in love fearlessly and to have the best first date ever. She later said that the song, and the album, weren't about being unafraid. Instead, it's about knowing the risks and taking them anyway. *Fearless* is more pop than country, with lyrics that appeal to women and girls of all ages.

HIDDEN MESSAGE
I loved you before I met you

FUN FACT
Swift put hidden messages in the lyric booklet for fans in her first five albums. Lowercase or uppercase letters spell out a secret note with the meaning behind each song.

'Cause I don't know how it gets better than this / You take my hand and drag me head first / Fearless

WRITERS: SWIFT, ROSE
PRODUCERS: SWIFT, CHAPMAN

YOU BELONG WITH ME

"You Belong With Me" tells the story of girl in love with her best friend, but he's already in a relationship. Swift wrote the song after hearing one of her friends talking to his girlfriend on the phone. In the song, the singer tells the boy that his girlfriend is wrong for him. She doesn't appreciate him. In comparison, the narrator has been there for him, she's right in front of him, and she wants to be more than friends. She hopes and dreams that someday he'll wake up and realize that they belong together.

Can't you see that I'm the one / Who understands you? / Been here all along / So, why can't you see? / You belong with me

HIDDEN MESSAGE
Love is blind so you couldn't see me

WRITER: SWIFT
PRODUCERS: SWIFT, CHAPMAN

LOVE STORY

What if *Romeo and Juliet* had a happy ending? What if the greatest story of forbidden love could rise above the doubt, allowing the boy and the girl to run away together? Swift wrote "Love Story" when she was 17 and her parents wouldn't let her see a boy she liked. She imagined they could make it work by sneaking out together. Romeo would come to her rescue, pull out a ring, and propose. The love story ends with a happily ever after.

We were both young when I first saw you / I close my eyes and the flashback starts / I'm standin' there / On a balcony in summer air

HIDDEN MESSAGE
Someday I'll find this

FUN FACT

Fearless was Swift's first producer credit. She also wrote seven of the tracks on her own.

evermore symbolizes fall and winter, while *folklore* represents spring and summer.

EVERMORE

evermore is Swift's ninth studio album, and a sort of partner to *folklore*, which had come out just five months earlier. This album, like its sister, was a surprise to fans. Swift used Instagram to announce its release. Both *evermore* and *folklore* have a poetic feel that takes listeners on a dreamy journey. Some of the stories Swift tells intersect. Others are mirror images, flipping the narrative from one side of the story to the other. "And may it continue, evermore," Swift wrote.

ALBUM TRACK LIST

1. "willow"
2. "champagne problems"
3. "gold rush"
4. "'tis the d— season"
5. "tolerate it"
6. "no body, no crime" (feat. HAIM)
7. "happiness"
8. "dorothea"
9. "coney island" (feat. The National)
10. "ivy"
11. "cowboy like me"
12. "long story short"
13. "marjorie"
14. "closure"
15. "evermore" (feat. Bon Iver)

ALBUM NOTES

15 tracks
Original release date: December 11, 2020
Writers: Taylor Swift, Aaron Dessner, Bryce Dessner, William Bowery, Jack Antonoff, Justin Vernon
Producers: Taylor Swift, Aaron Dessner, Jack Antonoff, BJ Burton, James McAlister
Guests: HAIM, The National, Bon Iver

WRITERS: SWIFT, DESSNER
PRODUCER: DESSNER

'TIS THE D— SEASON

"'tis the d— season" delves into the possibility of a whirlwind relationship. The narrator has returned to her hometown and wants to rekindle a relationship she had left behind. The narrator knows it will only last the weekend, but spending time with the person could be a positive and nostalgic experience.

CONCERT CUTS

"'tis the d— season" was left off the original cut of *Taylor Swift: The Eras Tour*, as well as *(Taylor's Version)* of the movie. "'tis the d— season" was swapped with "no body, no crime" on nights HAIM opened the show. The film was shot on one of those nights.

Time flies, messy as the mud on your truck tires / Now I'm missing your smile, hear me out / We could just ride around / And the road not taken looks real good now / And it always leads to you in my hometown

THE SET LIST

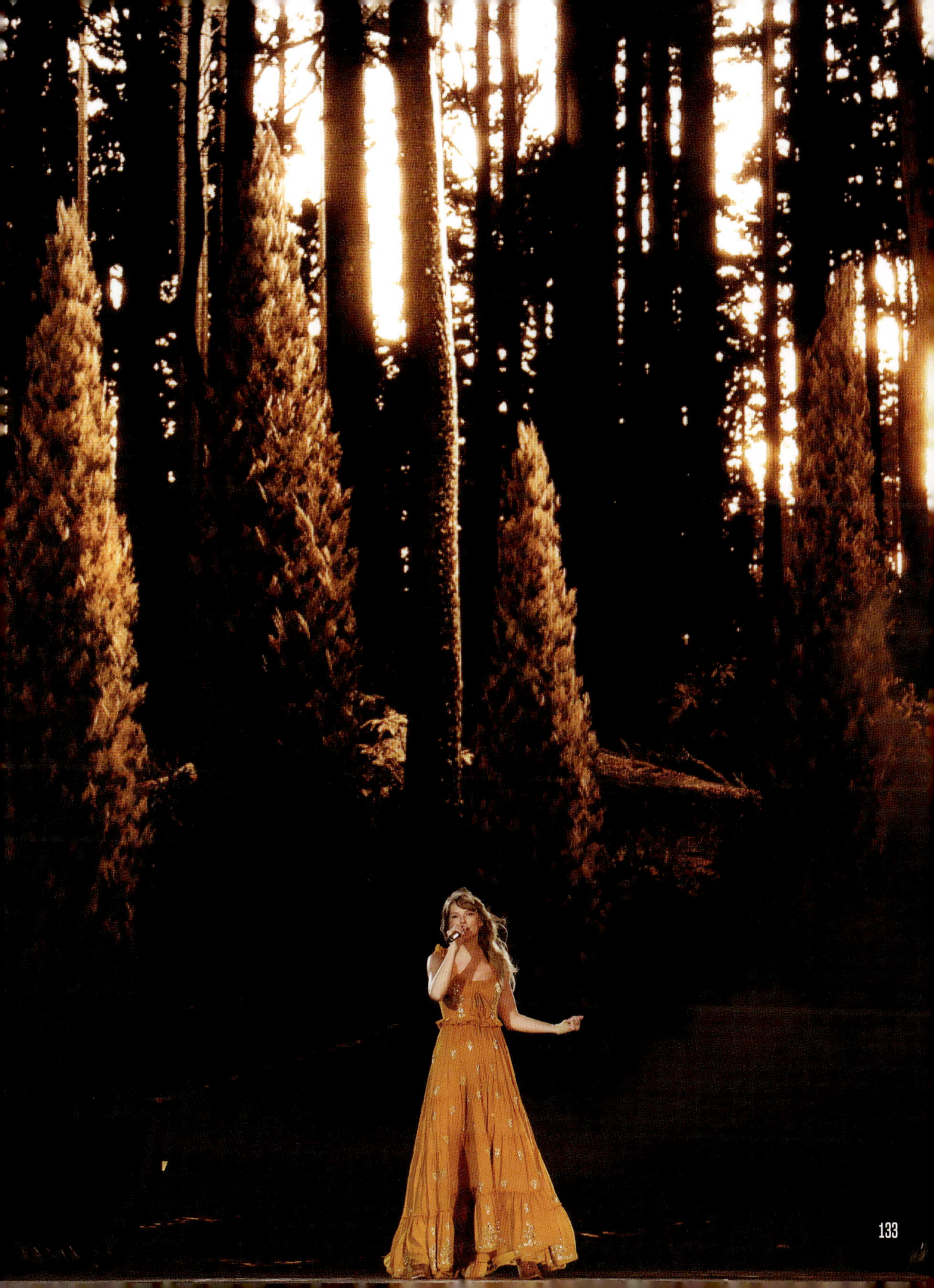

WRITERS: SWIFT, DESSNER
PRODUCER: DESSNER

WILLOW

"willow" was the first single released from *evermore*. It is about the desire and feelings that come along with wanting someone to fall in love with you. The lyrics are designed to pull the listener into the fantasy world Swift created. Swift says the song reminds her of casting a love spell.

FUN FACT

Before the release of the "willow" music video, Swift dropped some Easter eggs: "One scene represents how I feel about fame. There's a scene to represent each season throughout the journey of the video."

The more that you say / The less I know / Wherever you stray / I follow

THE SET LIST

WRITERS: SWIFT, DESSNER
PRODUCER: DESSNER

MARJORIE

The title of this song refers to Swift's maternal grandmother, Marjorie Finlay. Like Swift, Finlay was a singer. Holding a special place on track 13, "marjorie" opens with advice from Swift's grandmother. Swift sings about feeling as though her grandmother is still with her, playing a role in her life and supporting her decisions. Swift even uses sound clips of her grandmother's voice during the song.

*And if I didn't know better /
I'd think you were talking to me now /
If I didn't know better /
I'd think you were still around*

FUN FACT

The song "epiphany" is the 13th track on the *folklore* album. It is about Swift's paternal grandfather, Dean Swift.

FUN FACT

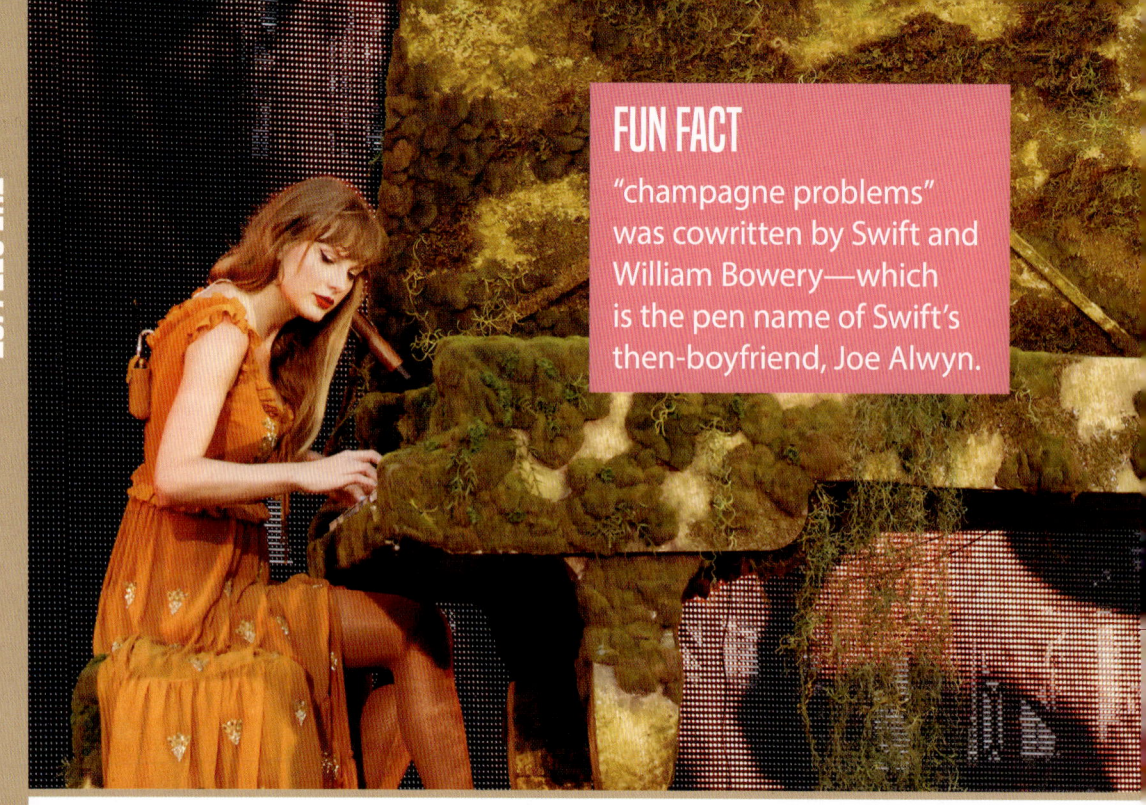

"champagne problems" was cowritten by Swift and William Bowery—which is the pen name of Swift's then-boyfriend, Joe Alwyn.

WRITERS: SWIFT, BOWERY
PRODUCERS: SWIFT, DESSNER

CHAMPAGNE PROBLEMS

"champagne problems" is the first part of a story that takes place in the *evermore* world. It revolves around a woman who rejects a marriage proposal. Heartbreak, sadness, and resilience are at its heart. Throughout the song, listeners are able to reflect on issues that seem simple but have big impacts on the people experiencing them. In the end, the narrator hopes her ex will go on to find someone new.

BIG, LITTLE PROBLEMS

The phrase "champagne problems" is used to describe problems that are trivial. The song discusses the end of a relationship and mental health. The narrator blames herself for creating what others might call champagne problems.

WRITERS: SWIFT, DESSNER
PRODUCER: DESSNER

TOLERATE IT

Swift was inspired by the movie *Rebecca* when she wrote "tolerate it." The main character marries a man whose first wife had mysteriously disappeared. She struggles, wondering if her husband cares about her at all. Swift's song explores the idea of being trapped in a relationship with an uncaring partner. The narrator has given the partnership her all, but has received nothing in return. And yet, she does not want to lose her partner, either. She's afraid to speak up in case it ends things forever.

If it's all in my head tell me now / Tell me I've got it wrong somehow / I know my love should be celebrated / But you tolerate it

REPUTATION

Reputation is Swift's response to the people who overanalyze her every word, every choice, and every relationship. She has been in the spotlight since the age of 15. Her sixth studio album let the haters know she had nothing to lose and was ready to control her story. Every song on the album has a different style, playing with darker tones, hip-hop, synth-pop, and music sampling while still giving fans tastes of classic Swift sounds.

There will be no future explanation. There will just be Reputation.

—SWIFT, REPUTATION BOOKLET

ALBUM NOTES

15 tracks

Original release date: November 10, 2017

Writers: Taylor Swift, Max Martin, Shellback, Ali Payami, Ed Sheeran, Nayvadius Wilburn, Jack Antonoff, Richard Fairbrass, Fred Fairbrass, Rob Manzoli, Oscar Görres, Oscar Holter

Producers: Taylor Swift, Max Martin, Shellback, Ali Payami, ILYA, Jack Antonoff, Oscar Görres, Oscar Holter

Guests: Ed Sheeran, Future

By 2018, *Reputation* had sold more than two million copies in the United States. It was the only album to do so in that time period.

ALBUM TRACK LIST

1. " . . . Ready For It?"
2. "End Game" (feat. Ed Sheeran and Future)
3. "I Did Something Bad"
4. "Don't Blame Me"
5. "Delicate"
6. "Look What You Made Me Do"
7. "So It Goes . . . "
8. "Gorgeous"
9. "Getaway Car"
10. "King of My Heart"
11. "Dancing with Our Hands Tied"
12. "Dress"
13. "This Is Why We Can't Have Nice Things"
14. "Call It What You Want"
15. "New Year's Day"

FUN FACT

Swift had executive produced her albums before, but *Reputation* was the first time she took full control of how her music would sound.

THE SET LIST

*Every love I've known in comparison is a failure /
I forget their names now, I'm so very tame now /
Never be the same now*

WRITERS: SWIFT, MARTIN, SHELLBACK, PAYAMI
PRODUCERS: MARTIN, SHELLBACK, PAYAMI

. . . READY FOR IT?

" . . . Ready For It?" is the first track on *Reputation*, and it let listeners know right away that the album was different from anything Taylor had done before. The lyrics are a reflection of getting past highly publicized relationships and moving on to become a stronger, more resilient person. The narrator has been with other people, learned lessons along the way, and is now ready to find her next partner in crime.

WRITERS: SWIFT, MARTIN, SHELLBACK
PRODUCERS: MARTIN, SHELLBACK

DELICATE

"Delicate" is an exploration of a relationship where one partner is highly scrutinized by the public. The song's romance is new and fragile. The song opens with the narrator informing her new partner about her current reputation. At the time, Swift was in a feud with Kanye, now known as Ye, and his then-wife, Kim Kardashian. Ye had released a song and recording that tarnished Swift's reputation. Swift's personal life—and her reputation—had never been more delicate.

My reputation's never been worse / So you must like me for me

WRITERS: SWIFT, MARTIN, SHELLBACK
PRODUCERS: MARTIN, SHELLBACK

THE SET LIST

DON'T BLAME ME

"Don't Blame Me" plays with the public perception of a boy-crazy Swift who was always the victim. The narrator of the song is addicted to a new man and admits she has a history of falling too hard. The sound is dark and broody, echoing the intensity of the lyrics.

Reputation was the first time Swift included swear words in her music.

Don't blame me, love made me crazy / If it doesn't, you ain't doin' it right

WRITERS: SWIFT, ANTONOFF, R. FAIRBRASS, F. FAIRBRASS, MANZOLI
PRODUCERS: SWIFT, ANTONOFF

LOOK WHAT YOU MADE ME DO

A song to critics and haters, "Look What You Made Me Do" is full of hidden messages, taking shots at celebrity feuds and hinting at karma coming around to those who have wronged Swift. A phone recording plays over part of the song, telling the caller that "the old Taylor can't come to the phone right now." Swift had shed her old skin and emerged fresh and new. She had fallen for cruel tricks in the past and realized no one could be trusted.

But I got smarter, I got harder in the nick of time / Honey, I rose up from the dead, I do it all the time

SPEAK NOW

Speak Now is Swift's third studio album. It was inspired by her transition between adolescence and adulthood. She wrote it herself and was also the only executive producer listed on the rerecording.

Many of the *Speak Now* songs are about heartbreak, rather than the more optimistic outlooks of love found on *Taylor Swift* or *Fearless*. There are also songs that deal with fame and the criticism that comes with success.

ALBUM TRACK LIST

1. "Mine"
2. "Sparks Fly"
3. "Back to December"
4. "Speak Now"
5. "Dear John"
6. "Mean"
7. "The Story of Us"
8. "Never Grow Up"
9. "Enchanted"
10. "Better than Revenge"
11. "Innocent"
12. "Haunted"
13. "Last Kiss"
14. "Long Live"

FUN FACT

Swift wrote *Speak Now* by herself while on tour. She treated each song as a diary entry, using the lyrics to help her deal with the emotions she felt as she grew into adulthood.

ALBUM NOTES

14 tracks

Original release date: October 25, 2010

Writer: Taylor Swift

Producers: Taylor Swift, Nathan Chapman

WRITER: SWIFT
PRODUCERS: SWIFT, CHAPMAN

ENCHANTED

"Enchanted" is a song about the excitement the narrator feels after meeting a new love interest for the first time. Will a small moment experienced between two people turn into something bigger? Swift wrote the song after meeting a mystery man in New York. She wondered if they would ever cross paths again. The song's lyrics are reminiscent of fairy tales.

PASSING NOTES IN SECRECY

In 2011, musician Adam Young realized "Enchanted" was about him. Swift had spelled out ADAM in the liner notes and, eventually, he figured it out. Young responded, creating a cover version of the song but changing some of the words: "I was enchanted to meet you, too," he sang.

WRITER: SWIFT
PRODUCERS: SWIFT, CHAPMAN

LONG LIVE

"Long Live" is a song to Swift's producers, musicians, friends, and fans who helped her in her *Fearless* era. The lyrics are like looking at snapshots of all her big musical moments, from award shows to concerts. It is a love song dedicated to Swifties everywhere.

I said, "Remember this moment" / In the back of my mind / The time we stood with our shaking hands / The crowds in stands went wild

FUN FACT

On June 6, 2023, reports confirmed that Swift's koi fish guitar had been temporarily removed from its place in the Country Music Hall of Fame. The next day, Swift revealed the guitar on night one in Kansas City. She used it to play "Long Live." The song got a permanent spot on the set list to celebrate the release of *Speak Now (Taylor's Version)*.

RED

Red is Swift's fourth studio album. It was inspired by the events and emotions Swift felt while on the Speak Now World Tour. She wanted to break out of her traditional songwriting practices and try something new. Swift's personal growth is evident in her desire to push herself creatively as a singer and a songwriter through *Red's* more mature song subjects.

Red is a mixture of different rock music styles. Swift spoke to musicians whose work she admired. New producers offered different sounds, adding diversity to Swift's emotional lyrics.

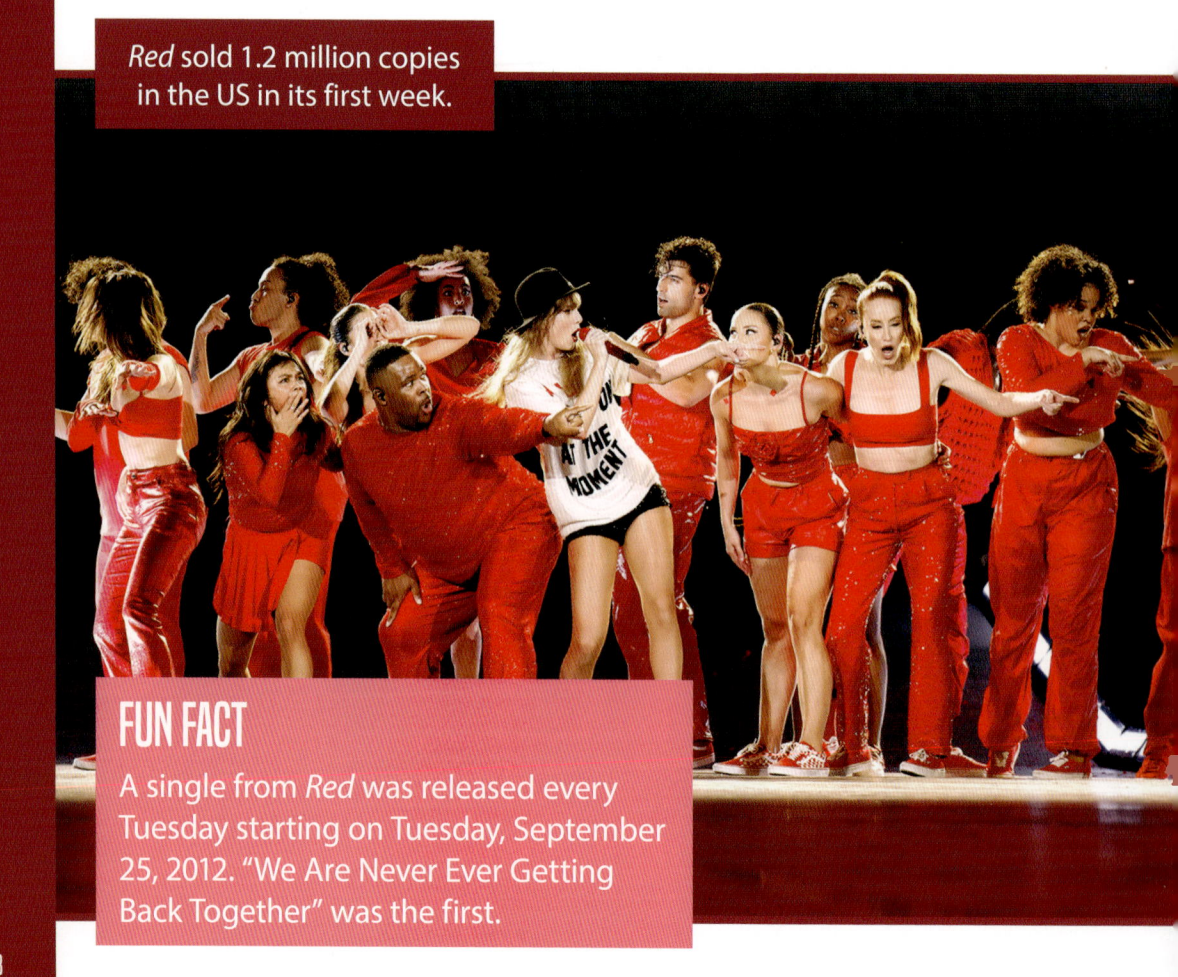

Red sold 1.2 million copies in the US in its first week.

FUN FACT

A single from *Red* was released every Tuesday starting on Tuesday, September 25, 2012. "We Are Never Ever Getting Back Together" was the first.

ALBUM NOTES

16 tracks

Original release date: October 22, 2012

Writers: Taylor Swift, Dan Wilson, Max Martin, Shellback, Liz Rose, Gary Lightbody, Jacknife Lee, Ed Sheeran

Producers: Taylor Swift, Nathan Chapman, Dann Huff, Dan Wilson, Shellback, Max Martin, Jacknife Lee, Jeff Bhasker, Butch Walker

Guests: Gary Lightbody, Ed Sheeran

ALBUM TRACK LIST

1. "State of Grace"
2. "Red"
3. "Treacherous"
4. "I Knew You Were Trouble"
5. "All Too Well"
6. "22"
7. "I Almost Do"
8. "We Are Never Ever Getting Back Together"
9. "Stay Stay Stay"
10. "The Last Time" (feat. Gary Lightbody)
11. "Holy Ground"
12. "Sad Beautiful Tragic"
13. "The Lucky One"
14. "Everything Has Changed" (feat. Ed Sheeran)
15. "Starlight"
16. "Begin Again"

THE SET LIST

WRITERS: SWIFT, MARTIN, SHELLBACK
PRODUCERS: MARTIN, SHELLBACK

22

"22" is about friends going out for the night, enjoying being young and carefree. It is about a time of growing up and taking on more responsibilities while still enjoying fun activities and dreaming big. It's a time of change—both good and bad.

We're happy, free, confused, and lonely in the best way / It's miserable and magical, oh, yeah

HIDDEN MESSAGE

Ashley Dianna
Claire Selena

THE SQUAD

Members of Taylor's friend group were called the squad. Actresses, singers, models, and other famous people have been part of this group. The names hidden in the liner note's secret message refer to Ashley Avignone, Dianna Agron, Claire Winter Kislinger, and Selena Gomez.

WRITERS: SWIFT, MARTIN, SHELLBACK
PRODUCERS: SWIFT, MARTIN, SHELLBACK

WE ARE NEVER EVER GETTING BACK TOGETHER

By the time *Red* came out, Swift was known as a sweet country singer. "We Are Never Ever Getting Back Together" was a huge departure from the twangy, banjo-accented ballads she was known for. It was catchy and the kind of song anyone who had ever gone through a breakup could relate to. Swift wrote it after being asked by someone if she was getting back with an ex.

RECORD SETTER

"We Are Never Ever Getting Back Together" set a Guinness World Record for being the fastest-selling single in digital history. It took just 50 minutes for it to reach the number-one spot on the iTunes singles sales chart. It was also Swift's first song to go number one.

HIDDEN MESSAGE

When I stopped caring what you thought

THE SET LIST

WRITERS: SWIFT, MARTIN, SHELLBACK
PRODUCERS: MARTIN, SHELLBACK

I KNEW YOU WERE TROUBLE

Swift wrote "I Knew You Were Trouble" after a breakup. It's a song about being heartbroken because the relationship is over, and upset that the relationship started in the first place. Obvious red flags should have warned the narrator. The song is a message to listeners to pay attention to their gut feelings.

FUN FACT

"I Knew You Were Trouble" was Swift's 50th Billboard Top 100 hit. Her first, "Tim McGraw" from *Taylor Swift*, had been released just six years and one month earlier.

I knew you were trouble when you walked in / So, shame on me now / Flew me to places I'd never been / Now I'm lyin' on the cold hard ground

HIDDEN MESSAGE

When you saw me dancing

WRITER: SWIFT
PRODUCERS: SWIFT, DESSNER
GUEST ARTIST: PHOEBE BRIDGERS

NOTHING NEW

If "22" is about the joy of getting older, "Nothing New" is about the fear of aging, especially in an industry that values youthfulness. The sound is indie rock. Phoebe Bridgers, who is a guest vocalist on the track, is one of the top artists of that genre. The song, written in 2012, is featured on Swift's 2021 album *Red (Taylor's Version)*. The song has been featured at select shows.

> And I wake up in the middle of the night / It's like I can feel time moving / How can a person know everything at 18 but nothing at 22? / Will you still want me / When I'm nothing new?

WRITERS: SWIFT, ROSE
PRODUCERS: SWIFT, CHAPMAN

THE SET LIST

ALL TOO WELL (10 MINUTE VERSION)

"All Too Well" was written during a hard time in Swift's personal life. She showed up at a rehearsal and started playing the same four chords again and again. The rest of the band started playing along. Swift added soulful lyrics to express what she was going through. Eventually, the song developed into "All Too Well." The song summarizes everything Taylor remembers all too well from a past relationship. It is the perfect example of Swift's incredible gift for storytelling.

'Cause there we are again on that little town street / You almost ran the red 'cause you were lookin' over at me / Wind in my hair, I was there / I remember it all too well

FUN FACT

The original version of "All Too Well" is 5 minutes, 29 seconds long. The longer version is 10 minutes, 13 seconds.

HIDDEN MESSAGE

Maple Latte

10 MIN, 13 SEC

Swift did not initially release the 10 minute version of "All Too Well." Fans begged Swift to release it. When Swift rerecorded *Red (Taylor's Version)*, the full song was added to the track list.

FOLKLORE

Swift spent the COVID-19 lockdown writing music. Fans had gotten *Lover* less than a year before, but *folklore*—and *evermore*, which would be released five months later—had a completely different tone. Swift leaned away from poppy, radio-friendly tunes and instead embraced the power of her songwriting. *folklore* is solemn and dreamy, telling stories about characters made up by Swift. The album is comforting and contemplative, allowing listeners to reflect inward, away from the stress and anxiety caused by a global pandemic.

folklore was the best-selling album of 2020, with 1.3 million copies purchased on the day of its release.

FUN FACT

folklore and *evermore* were written and released in 2020 during the COVID-19 pandemic. That was also the year Swift turned 31, the mirror of her lucky number 13.

ALBUM NOTES

16 tracks
Original release date: July 24, 2020
Writers: Taylor Swift, Aaron Dessner, William Bowery, Justin Vernon, Jack Antonoff
Producers: Taylor Swift, Aaron Dessner, Jack Antonoff, Joe Alwyn
Guest artist: Bon Iver

ALBUM TRACK LIST

1. "the 1"
2. "cardigan"
3. "the last great american dynasty"
4. "exile" (feat. Bon Iver)
5. "my tears ricochet"
6. "mirrorball"
7. "seven"
8. "august"
9. "this is me trying"
10. "illicit affairs"
11. "invisible string"
12. "mad woman"
13. "epiphany"
14. "betty"
15. "peace"
16. "hoax"

WRITERS: SWIFT, DESSNER
PRODUCER: DESSNER

INVISIBLE STRING

At the start of the tour, Swift opened her *folklore* Era with "invisible string." It is a love song about the thread of fate that ties soulmates together. The song lyrics are reflective. The narrator has grown from past heartbreak and is looking forward to the possibility of a healthy relationship.

And isn't it just so pretty to think / All along there was some / Invisible string / Tying you to me?

THE STRINGS BETWEEN US

The Invisible String theory is the idea that the universe connects people before they're destined to meet. An example would be a couple being at the same birthday party in elementary school years before meeting.

We never painted by the numbers, baby / But we were making it count / You know the greatest loves of all time are over now

WRITERS: SWIFT, DESSNER
PRODUCER: DESSNER

THE 1

"the 1" replaced "invisible string" on the set list on March 31, 2023, in Arlington, Texas. "the 1" is about a relationship that's over. If it had worked out, though, the partner could have been "the one." But it didn't, so they're not. The lyrics reflect on lost love, regrets, and the nostalgia of happy memories.

FUN FACT

It was reported that Swift and Alwyn parted ways during the first part of the Eras Tour. "the 1" replaced "invisible string" in the set list after the breakup but before fans officially knew.

WRITERS: SWIFT, BOWERY
PRODUCERS: SWIFT, DESSNER, ANTONOFF, ALWYN

BETTY

folklore has three songs about a love triangle. "betty" is one. "cardigan" and "august" are the others. "betty" is told from the point of view of James, a teenage boy who cheated on his girlfriend Betty during summer vacation. When they return to school, James finds it hard to see Betty again. He realizes how much he regrets his actions. James ends up genuinely apologizing to Betty for what he has done.

You heard the rumors from Inez / You can't believe a word she says / Most times, but this time, it was true / The worst thing that I ever did was what I did to you

WRITERS: SWIFT, DESSNER
PRODUCER: DESSNER

THE LAST GREAT AMERICAN DYNASTY

The song "the last great american dynasty" chronicles the life of Rebekah Harkness, a real-life socialite who lived life on her own terms. She was one of the richest women of the 20th century. Harkness was married four times, threw lavish parties at her mansion, and did it all without caring what other people thought. Harkness and Swift live in ways that raise eyebrows and defy society.

THEY PICKED OUT A HOME

During her lifetime, Harkness owned a huge mansion in Rhode Island called Holiday House. Swift bought Holiday House in 2013 after learning about Harkness. The two share many similarities, such as their fame, fortune, and reputation among gossipers. The last stanza of "the last great american dynasty" could describe either woman.

Holiday House sat quietly on that beach / Free of women with madness, their men and bad habits / And then it was bought by me

WRITERS: SWIFT, ANTONOFF
PRODUCERS: SWIFT, ANTONOFF, ALWYN

AUGUST

"august" is the story of the teenage love triangle from the "other woman's" perspective. She is unnamed, although some fans call her Augustine. The summer fling has come to an end and she realizes how unimportant she was to James. She was young, infatuated, and desperate for James to notice her but eventually sees that he was never hers.

But I can see us lost in the memory / August slipped away into a moment in time / 'Cause it was never mine

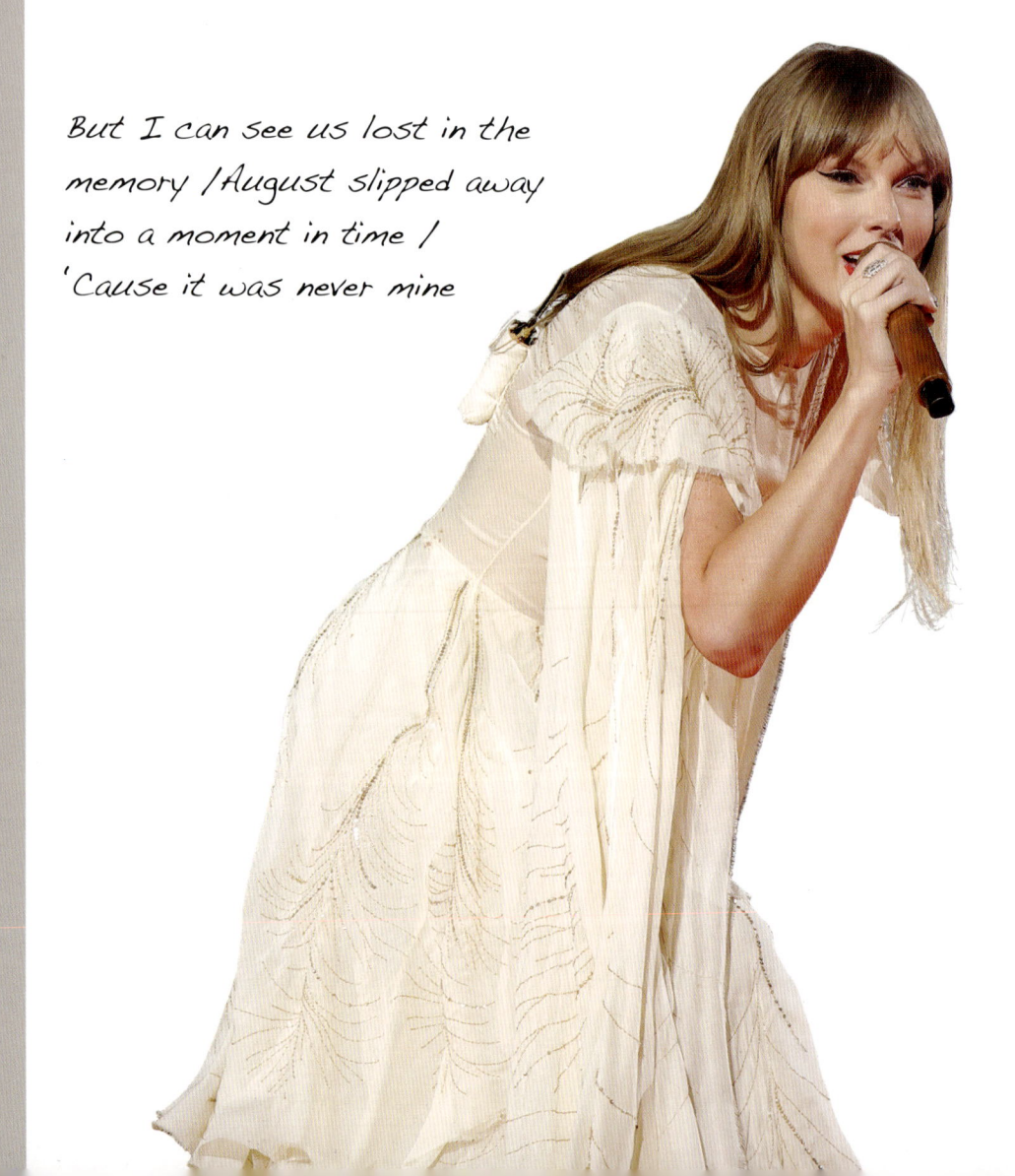

Don't call me "kid" / Don't call me "baby" / Look at this idiotic fool that you made me / You taught me a secret language / I can't speak with anyone else

WRITERS: SWIFT, ANTONOFF
PRODUCERS: SWIFT, ANTONOFF, ALWYN

ILLICIT AFFAIRS

Swift takes listeners deep into a secret affair full of love, lies, and longing. The excitement of feeling wanted and desired is contrasted by rejection, embarrassment, and shame. It's a song about love that can never be public, narrated by a person who isn't sure how to feel about the chaotic relationship.

WRITER: SWIFT
PRODUCERS: SWIFT, ANTONOFF, ALWYN

THE SET LIST

MY TEARS RICOCHET

"my tears ricochet" is the fifth track on *folklore,* a spot often reserved for highly emotional songs. The lyrics describe someone showing up at the funeral of a person they once loved. It's both about the death of a person and a relationship.

A different look at the words reveals the battle between Big Machine Records and Swift for the rights to her music. The conflict soured the once-healthy relationship between Swift and the label.

You know I didn't want to have to haunt you / But what a ghostly scene / You wear the same jewels that I gave you / As you bury me

"my tears ricochet" was the first song Swift wrote for *folklore.*

A friend to all is a friend to none / Chase two girls, lose the one / When you are young, they assume you know nothin'

WRITERS: SWIFT, DESSNER
PRODUCER: DESSNER

CARDIGAN

"cardigan" tells the story of the love triangle from Betty's perspective. Betty is older now, looking back at what happened. She remembers being insecure, but James made her feel safe. Betty knew after they broke up that she would feel the betrayal for years. She found a way to forgive him but could never forget.

THE SET LIST

1989

Swift's fifth studio album was written while she was on tour for *Red*. That album had been a country-pop crossover, and critics had argued about whether Swift was really a country singer. *1989* showed the haters that Swift could do both. Its sound is based off of 1980s synth-pop, utilizing synthesizer keyboards, drum machines, and music sequencers. The vibe is completely different from Swift's previous work, which relies heavily on acoustic guitars. Fans loved the catchy, upbeat tunes.

ALBUM TRACK LIST

1. "Welcome to New York"
2. "Blank Space"
3. "Style"
4. "Out of the Woods"
5. "All You Had to Do Was Stay"
6. "Shake It Off"
7. "I Wish You Would"
8. "Bad Blood"
9. "Wildest Dreams"
10. "How You Get the Girl"
11. "This Love"
12. "I Know Places"
13. "Clean"

1989 (Taylor's version) sold nearly 1.3 million copies during its opening week.

ALBUM NOTES

13 tracks
Original release date: October 27, 2014
Writers: Taylor Swift, Ryan Tedder, Max Martin, Shellback, Ali Payami, Jack Antonoff, Imogen Heap
Producers: Taylor Swift, Ryan Tedder, Noel Zancanella, Shellback, Ali Payami, Jack Antonoff, Max Martin, Mattman & Robin, Greg Kurstin, Nathan Chapman, Imogen Heap

WRITERS: SWIFT, MARTIN, SHELLBACK, PAYAMI
PRODUCERS: MARTIN, SHELLBACK, PAYAMI

STYLE

"Style" tackles an on-and-off again relationship. The couple can't quit each other despite knowing the relationship probably won't work. Their love will never go out of style. Swift wrote it thinking about the old clothes in her closet that she couldn't bring herself to throw away. Sometimes, love is timeless and worth trying, even if it's not always perfect. "Style" is one of the earlier examples of Swift deviating from romantic love stories and instead addressing the messier aspects of adult relationships.

> You got that James Dean daydream look in your eye / And I got that red lip classic thing that you like / And when we go crashing down, we come back every time / 'Cause we never go out of style, we never go out of style

WRITERS: SWIFT, MARTIN, SHELLBACK
PRODUCERS: MARTIN, SHELLBACK

BLANK SPACE

Being in the public eye means Swift's private life has never been her own. Her early breakup anthems were analyzed with great detail. "Blank Space" shows fans that Swift is fully aware of her reputation and can make fun of herself and the media at the same time. It also points out the double standard in the coverage of men and women in the media.

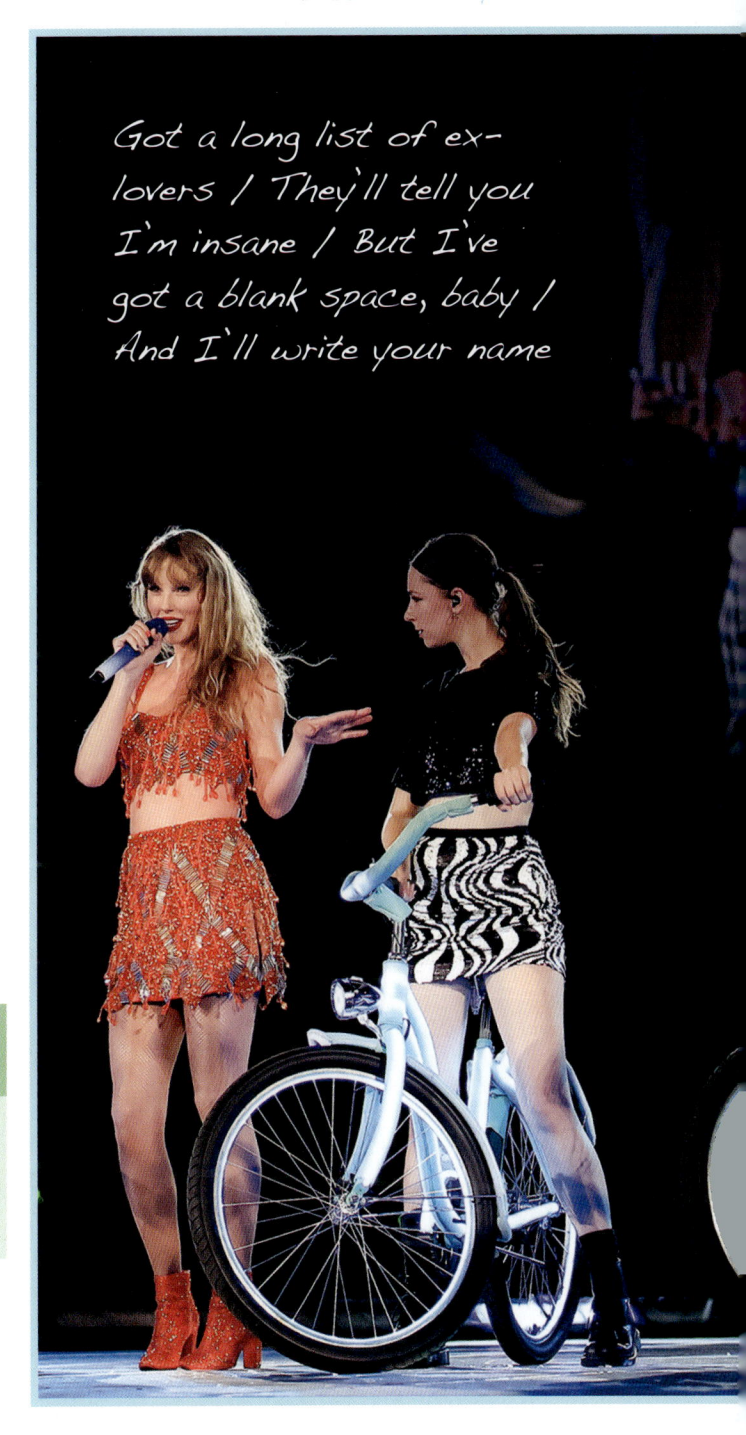

Got a long list of ex-lovers / They'll tell you I'm insane / But I've got a blank space, baby / And I'll write your name

HIDDEN MESSAGE

There once was a girl known by everyone and no one

THE SET LIST

WRITERS: SWIFT, MARTIN, SHELLBACK
PRODUCERS: MARTIN, SHELLBACK

SHAKE IT OFF

"Shake It Off" was the first single released from *1989*, and fully it launched Taylor's move from country to pop. The up-tempo song guides listeners to take back their own stories and not to let other people get under their skin. Ignore the haters. Dance instead!

FUN FACT

"Shake It Off" was Swift's second number-one Billboard Top 100 hit.

But I keep cruisin' / Can't stop, won't stop movin' / It's like I got this music in my mind / Sayin' it's gonna be alright

HIDDEN MESSAGE

She danced to forget him

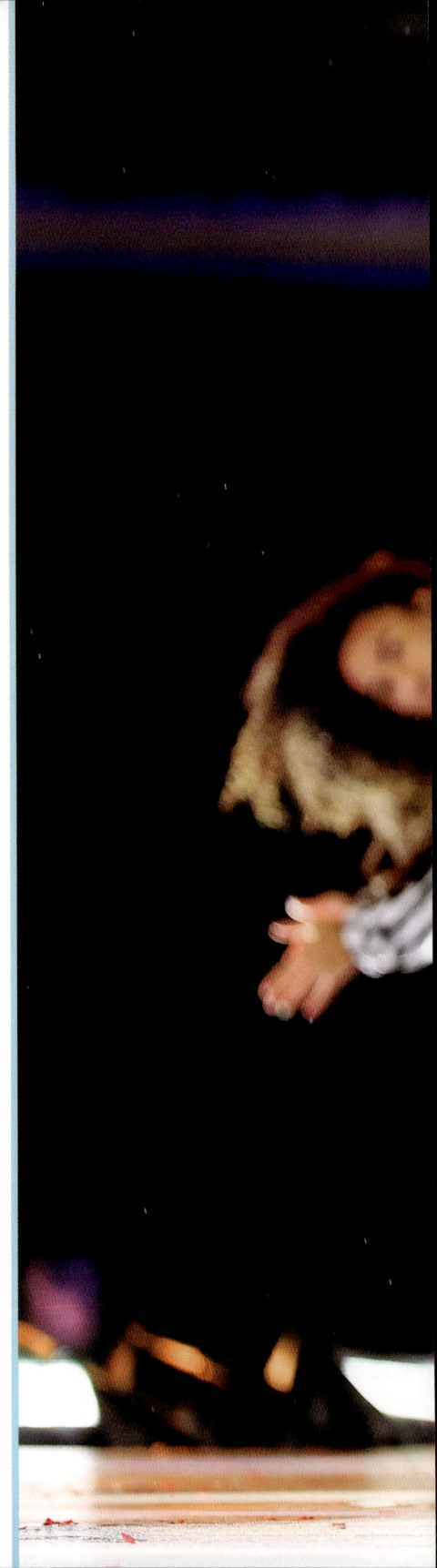

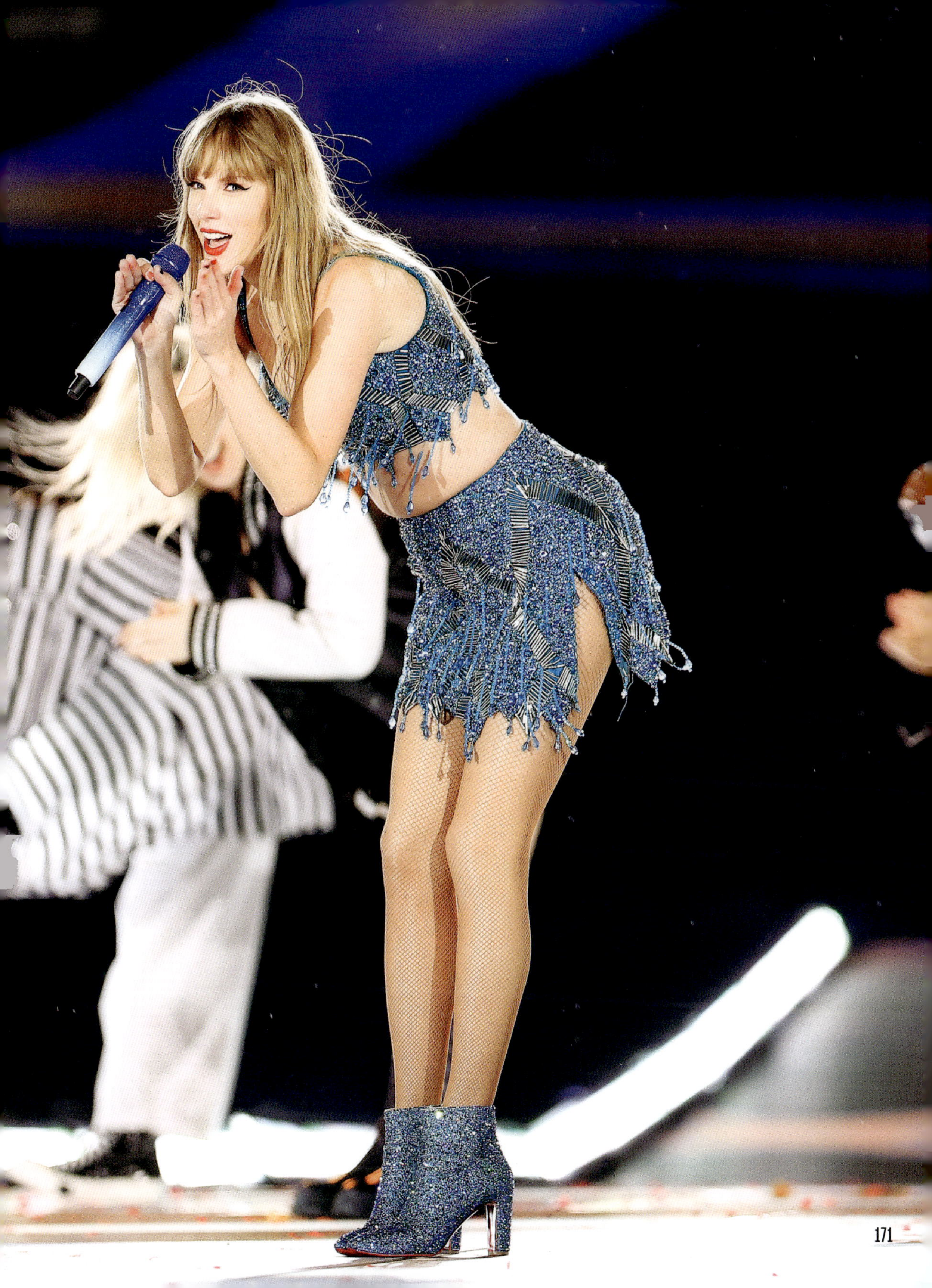

THE SET LIST

WRITERS: SWIFT, MARTIN, SHELLBACK
PRODUCERS: MARTIN, SHELLBACK

WILDEST DREAMS

Starting a relationship is hard, but ending one can be even harder. The narrator of "Wildest Dreams" knows from the beginning that the dreamy relationship will have to end, but wants to get the most out of it that she can. She also doesn't want her partner to forget about her. The wildest dream is that their love will be worth remembering.

Someday when you leave me / I bet these memories / Follow you around

HIDDEN MESSAGE
He only saw her in his dreams

FUN FACT
Swift sampled her own heartbeat for "Wildest Dreams."

Now we got problems / And I don't think we can solve 'em / You made a really deep cut / And baby, now we got bad blood, hey

> **HIDDEN MESSAGE**
>
> She made friends and enemies

WRITERS: SWIFT, MARTIN, SHELLBACK
PRODUCERS: MARTIN, SHELLBACK

BAD BLOOD

Swift is known for her relationship ballads. However, songs about friendships—and friendships gone bad—are also part of her frequently touched-upon subjects. "Bad Blood" addresses a feud Taylor had with another famous music star. According to reports, the other singer tried to hire Swift's backup dancers in the middle of a tour. Swift said "Bad Blood" wasn't about calling the other person out. It was a song that other people could apply to their own lives.

SURPRISE SONGS

At every show, Swift plays two surprise songs, one on acoustic guitar and one on acoustic piano. Originally, Swift intended to play each surprise song only once, unless she made a mistake while performing or it was on *Midnights*. In 2024, she announced that she would start the list over again, which pleased fans who hadn't yet seen the show.

> The first surprise songs after resetting the list were mash-ups of "Tim McGraw/Cowboy Like Me" and "Mirrorball/Epiphany."

TAYLOR SWIFT

"Tim McGraw"
"Picture to Burn"
"Teardrops On My Guitar"
"A Place in this World"
"Cold As You"
"Tied Together With a Smile"
"Stay Beautiful"
"Should've Said No"
"Our Song"
"I'm Only Me When I'm With You"
"Invisible"

FEARLESS

"Fifteen"
"Hey Stephen"
"White Horse"
"Breathe"
"Tell Me Why"
"You're Not Sorry"
"Forever & Always"
"Jump Then Fall"
"Untouchable"
"The Other Side of the Door"
"Today Was a Fairytale"
"You All Over Me"
"Mr. Perfectly Fine" *

FUN FACT

Swift performed "Last Kiss" for the surprise song on night two in Kansas City. It was July ninth, the date mentioned in the lyrics. Swift messed up the words in the second verse, laughed it off, and started from the beginning.

SPEAK NOW

"Mine"
"Sparks Fly"
"Back to December"
"Speak Now"
"Dear John"
"Mean"
"The Story of Us"
"Never Grow Up"
"Better Than Revenge"
"Innocent"
"Haunted"
"Last Kiss"
"Ours"
"If This Was a Movie"
"When Emma Falls in Love" *
"I Can See You" *
"Castles Crumbling" *
"Timeless" *

RED

"State of Grace"
"Red"
"Treacherous"
"I Almost Do"
"Stay Stay Stay"
"The Last Time"
"Holy Ground"
"Sad Beautiful Tragic"
"The Lucky One"
"Everything Has Changed"
"Starlight"
"Begin Again"
"The Moment I Knew"
"Come Back . . . Be Here" *
"Better Man"
"Message In a Bottle" *
"I Bet You Think About Me" *
"The Very First Night"

(*denotes the title is from Taylor's Version)

THE SET LIST

1989

"Welcome to New York"
"Out of the Woods"
"All You Had to Do Was Stay"
"I Wish You Would"
"How You Get the Girl"
"This Love"
"I Know Places"
"Clean"
"Wonderland"
"You Are in Love"
"New Romantics"
"S—!" *
"Say Don't Go" *
"Now That We Don't Talk" *
"Suburban Legends" *
"Is It Over Now?" *

REPUTATION

"End Game"
"So It Goes . . ."
"Gorgeous"
"Getaway Car"
"King of My Heart"
"Dancing With Our Hands Tied"
"Dress"
"This Is Why We Can't Have Nice Things"
"Call It What You Want"
"New Year's Day"

LOVER

"I Forgot That You Existed"
"I Think He Knows"
"Paper Rings"
"Cornelia Street"
"Death by a Thousand Cuts"
"False God"
"Afterglow"
"ME!"
"Daylight"
"All Of the Girls You Loved Before"

FOLKLORE

"exile"
"mirrorball"
"this is me trying"
"mad woman"
"the lakes"

EVERMORE

"gold rush"
"no body, no crime"
"dorothea"
"coney island"
"ivy"
"cowboy like me"
"evermore"
"right where you left me"
"it's time to go"

FUN FACT

"Safe & Sound" is a song from the movie soundtrack *The Hunger Games: Songs from District 12 and Beyond*. It played during the movie's credits.

MIDNIGHTS

"Maroon"
"Snow on the Beach"
"You're On Your Own, Kid"
"Question . . . ?"
"Labyrinth"
"Sweet Nothing"
"The Great War"
"Bigger Than the Whole Sky"
"High Infidelity"
"Would've, Could've, Should've"
"Hits Different"

MISCELLANEOUS

"I Don't Wanna Live Forever"
"I miss you, I'm sorry" (with Gracie Abrams)
"Safe & Sound"

Fans all over the world kept track of Swift's set list and compared how each show differed.

MIDNIGHTS

Swift wrote *Midnights* during a string of sleepless nights. Her songs have five themes: falling in love, falling apart, revenge fantasies, self-loathing, and wondering what might have been. As with some of her other albums, the songs touch on fame and how it affects Swift's life. The sound is a mixture of electronica, R&B, and hip-hop, with Swift's deep, breathy voice layered on top of itself between cadenced beats.

Midnights was Swift's 11th number-one album in a row on the Billboard 200 list. It was also the best-selling album of 2022.

ALBUM NOTES

13 tracks
Original release date: October 21, 2022
Writers: Taylor Swift, Jack Antonoff, Zoë Kravitz, Lana Del Rey, Mark Spears, Jahaan Sweet, Sam Dew, William Bowery, Keanu Torres
Producers: Taylor Swift, Jack Antonoff, Sounwave, Jahan Sweet, Braxton Cook, Keanu Torres
Guest: Lana Del Rey

FUN FACT

With *Midnights*, Swift became the first artist in history to hold the top 10 spots on the Billboard Hot 100. *Midnights* also became the first album to have 10 top 10 songs.

ALBUM TRACK LIST

1. "Lavender Haze"
2. "Maroon"
3. "Anti-Hero"
4. "Snow on the Beach" (feat. Lana Del Rey)
5. "You're on Your Own, Kid"
6. "Midnight Rain"
7. "Question . . . ?"
8. "Vigilante S—"
9. "Bejeweled"
10. "Labyrinth"
11. "Karma"
12. "Sweet Nothing"
13. "Mastermind"

WRITERS: SWIFT, ANTONOFF, KRAVITZ, SPEARS, SWEET, DEW
PRODUCERS: SWIFT, ANTONOFF, SOUNWAVE, SWEET, COOK

LAVENDER HAZE

"Lavender Haze" is a violet dream, calling to mind romance and cloudy skies. The term "lavender haze" was first used in the 1950s. It describes the early, glowing love at the beginning of a serious relationship. The narrator speaks from a cloud of that lavender haze, doing everything she can to keep the outside world away.

I just wanna stay in that lavender haze

I have this thing where I get older but just never wiser / Midnights become my afternoons

WRITERS: SWIFT, ANTONOFF
PRODUCERS: SWIFT, ANTONOFF

ANTI-HERO

"Anti-Hero" pits Swift against her biggest enemy—herself. It's a list of things Swift dislikes about herself, in a brutally honest, self-deprecating way. The chorus, "It's me, hi, I'm the problem, it's me," resonates with listeners everywhere. Getting older but never growing out of destructive behaviors, sabotaging relationships, and taking responsibility for life spiraling out of control are things many people can relate to.

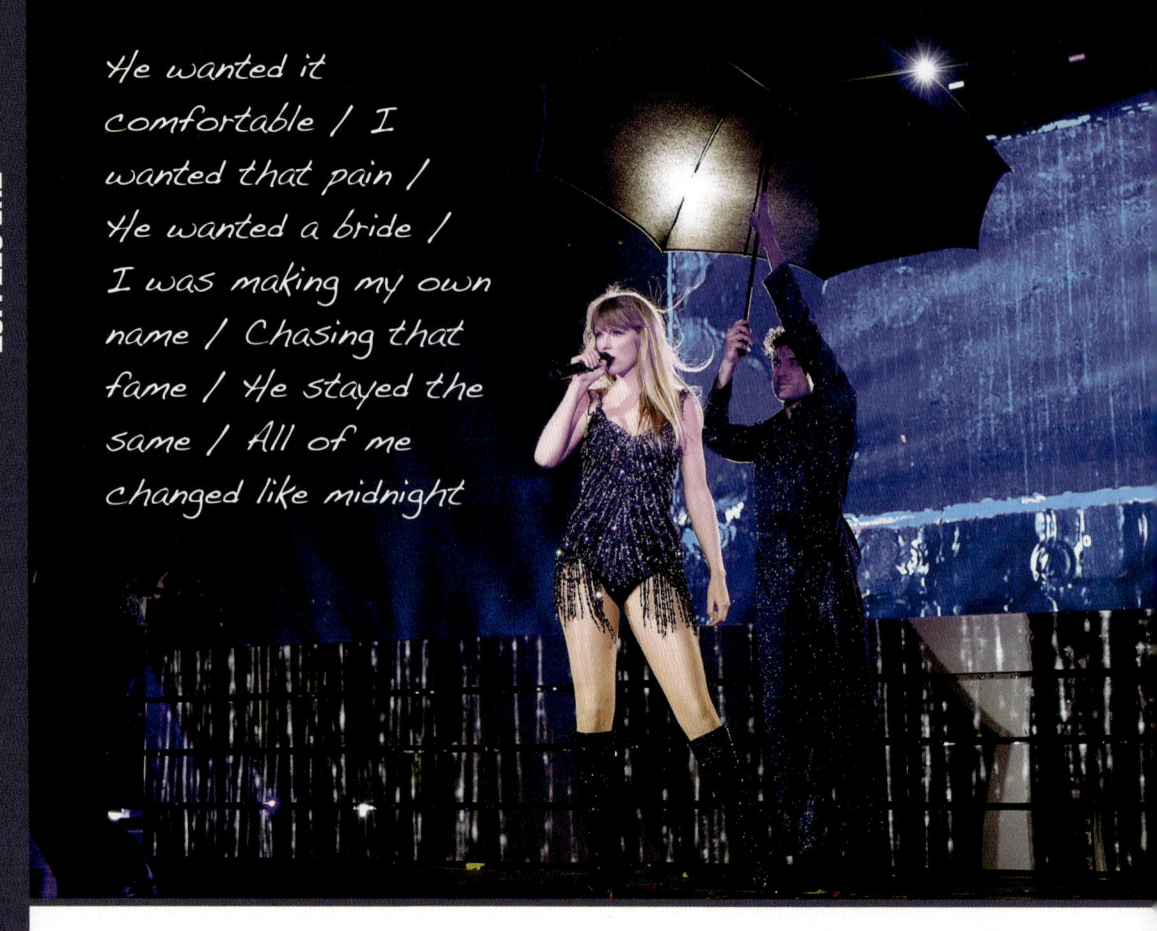

He wanted it comfortable / I wanted that pain / He wanted a bride / I was making my own name / Chasing that fame / He stayed the same / All of me changed like midnight

WRITERS: SWIFT, ANTONOFF
PRODUCERS: SWIFT, ANTONOFF

MIDNIGHT RAIN

If "Lavender Haze" describes the glow of two people at the start of a relationship, "Midnight Rain" describes the relationship's demise. The narrator is caught between her career and her relationship and needs to choose between the two, even though she knows exactly what she wants.

FUN FACT

In February 2024, Swift won her fourth Album of the Year Grammy for *Midnights*. She became the first and only female solo artist to achieve this.

WRITER: SWIFT
PRODUCERS: SWIFT, ANTONOFF

VIGILANTE S—

Swift has written songs about what happened between her and record executive Scooter Braun before. Her rerecordings are an act of rebellion against him for selling her songs. "Vigilante S—" lists crimes and the ways the singer gets mad—and gets even. The sound of vengeance is cool and dark, with hip-hop tones over trap beats and drum melodies.

I don't start it but I can tell you how it ends / Don't get sad, get even

FUN FACT
Swift is the sole writer of her song "Vigilante S—."

WRITERS: SWIFT, ANTONOFF
PRODUCERS: SWIFT, ANTONOFF

BEJEWELED

Swift spent time writing mellow ballads for *folklore* and *evermore*. "Bejeweled" returned her to the world of bubblegum pop, with an upbeat sound and lyrics. In the song, the narrator realizes how much she dulled her shine to please her partner. She warns her partner that she will no longer do that. The song's message is to know your value and to demand the treatment you deserve.

Best believe I'm still bejeweled / When I walk in the room / I can still make the whole place shimmer

WRITERS: SWIFT, ANTONOFF
PRODUCERS: SWIFT, ANTONOFF

MASTERMIND

"Mastermind" is the final song on the *Midnights* album. It is an origin story and a tale of how the narrator helped things fall into place to begin a romance. The song progresses to be more directly about Swift. It references how hard she worked to be loved by the public. "Mastermind" celebrates Swift's hard work in love and life.

What if I told you none of it was accidental / And the first night that you saw me, nothing was gonna stop me? / I laid the groundwork and then, just like clockwork / The dominoes cascaded in a line / What if I told you I'm a mastermind?

FUN FACT

On February 5, 2024, Swift announced she was dropping a new album, *The Tortured Poets Department*, on April 19.

Ask me what I learned from all those years / Ask me what I earned from all those tears / Ask me why so many fade, but I'm still here

KARMA

WRITERS: SWIFT, ANTONOFF, SWEET, TORRES, SPEARS
PRODUCERS: SWIFT, ANTONOFF, SWEET, TORRES, SOUNWAVE

Swift uses "Karma" to end the journey through all of her Eras. The song is Swift's love letter to herself. It's about taking pride in life's good moments and reaping the rewards. The lyrics lead the audience toward the show's finale. Swift embraces the idea of learning from the disappointments and difficulties that come with years of hard work. It's time to celebrate her success!

KARMA IS COMING?

Since *Reputation*, Swifties speculated about a rumored lost album called *Karma*. As far back as 2016, Swift began talking about karma and working it into lyrics and interviews. She also started adding orange to some of her looks, as though she was setting up future hints and Easter eggs. Then, at the end of the Eras Tour concert, an orange door descends from the top of the stage.

GLOSSARY

array
An ordered series or arrangement.

asymmetrical
When both sides of something are not the same.

bespoke
Custom-made clothing.

Bluetooth
Short-range wireless technology used to send data between devices.

Bohemian
A fashion style that mixes different cultures, artistic expressions, patterns, and materials.

colorway
A range of colors available for a design or style.

debut
A first appearance or performance.

dynasty
A series of rulers from the same family.

economy
The system of how money is made and used within a particular country or region.

era
A period of history that can be measured.

genre
A category of music, literature, film, or other artistic work.

gross
The total amount made before paying taxes or other deductions.

inclusive
Including someone as part of a group.

infrared
Electromagnetic radiation used to send signals to entertainment devices.

LED
A device that can emit light when an electric current passes through it; LED stands for light emitting diode.

magnitude
The amount of energy released during an earthquake; the largest earthquake ever recorded reached 9.5 magnitude.

vigilante
A person who takes the law into their own hands.

waive
Choosing not to enforce something, such as fees or rules.

wash light
A light that bathes an area with soft beams of light.

TO LEARN MORE

FURTHER READINGS

Gottlieb, Beth. *Taylor Swift*. Enslow Publishing, 2024.

Newman, Terry. *Taylor Swift and the Clothes She Wears.* ACC Art Books, 2023.

Perricone, Kathleen. *Taylor Swift Is Life: A Superfan's Guide to All Things We Love about Taylor Swift.* Epic Ink, 2024.

ONLINE RESOURCES

Booklinks
NONFICTION NETWORK
FREE! ONLINE NONFICTION RESOURCES

To learn more about Taylor Swift, please visit **abdobooklinks.com** or scan this QR code. These links are routinely monitored and updated to provide the most current information available.

INDEX

Agency, The, 37, 38, 53
Alberta Ferretti 93, 94, 97, 98
"All Too Well" 154
"All Too Well (10 Minute Version)" 50, 91, 154
"Anti-Hero" 58, 181
Arlington, Texas 159
Ashish Gupta 86, 90, 91
Atelier Versace 60, 63
"august" 53, 160, 162
backup dancers 30, 32-35, 38, 40, 44, 46, 47, 50, 53, 54, 58, 59, 173
"Bad Blood" 55, 173
"Bejeweled" 23, 59, 184
"betty" 53, 160
"Blank Space" 54, 169
Bridgers, Phoebe 153
Buenos Aires, Argentina 63
Canada 18
"cardigan" 53, 160, 165
"champagne problems" 45, 136
Christian Louboutin 60, 64, 69, 86, 100, 109
"Cruel Summer" 41, 119
De Vincenzo, Marco 73
"Delicate" 38, 46, 141
"Don't Blame Me" 46, 142
Elie Saab 80, 83
"Enchanted" 48, 146
Etro 70, 73
evermore 70, 73, 130, 134, 136, 156, 176, 184
"Fearless" 126
Fearless 124 144, 147, 175
Finlay, Marjorie 135
folklore 53, 130, 156, 157, 158, 160, 164, 176, 184
Folklore Cabin 52, 53
friendship bracelets 23
Glendale, Arizona 10
Grammy Award 124

HAIM 24
Harkness, Rebekah 161
heart hands 20
"I Knew You Were Trouble" 50, 86, 152
"illicit affairs" 53, 163
"invisible string" 158, 159
Jones, Jessica 104, 107
"Karma" 59, 115, 186
Las Vegas 112
"Lavender Haze" 108, 180, 182
"Long Live" 147
"Look What You Made Me Do" 47, 143
Los Angeles 113
"Love Story" 128
"Lover" 122
Lover 116, 121, 156, 176
Lover House 41, 55
"marjorie" 45, 135
"Mastermind" 59, 185
"Mean" 121
Melbourne, Australia 14
"Midnight Rain" 182
Midnights 7, 174, 177, 178
Midnights (The Late Night Edition) 27
misc songs 177
"Miss Americana & the Heartbreak Prince" 41, 118
Moore, Mandy 30
"my tears ricochet" 53, 164
New Jersey 27, 63
Nicole + Felicia 76, 84, 85
1989 36, 103, 166, 170, 176
1989 (Taylor's Version) 85, 98
"Nothing New" 153
Oscar de la Renta 110, 112, 113
Paramore 24
Puglisi, Fausto 66, 100
"...Ready For It?" 46, 140
records 7, 14, 15, 29
Red 36, 148, 151, 166, 175

Red (Taylor's Version) 153
Reputation 36, 104, 118, 138, 140, 176
Reputation Stadium Tour 74
Roberto Cavalli 66, 69, 74, 100, 103, 107
"Shake It Off" 55, 170
Speak Now 76, 84, 89, 118, 121, 144, 175
Speak Now (Taylor's Version) 89
Speak Now World Tour 66, 89, 148
Starlights, The 36, 38, 53
"Style" 168
Swarovski 69, 100
Swifties 10, 20, 22, 23, 26, 119, 147
Sydney, Australia 14
Taylor Swift 4, 118, 126, 144, 175
"the 1" 159
"The Archer" 123
"the last great american dynasty" 53, 161
"The Man" 41, 64, 120
Ticketmaster 8, 14
"'tis the d— season" 132
"tolerate it" 45, 137
Toronto, Canada 18
"22" 50, 86, 88, 150, 153
"22" hat 23, 50, 86
Versace 64
"Vigilante S—" 59, 183
"We Are Never Ever Getting Back Together" 36, 50, 151
"Wildest Dreams" 172
"willow" 70, 134
"You Belong With Me" 43, 127
"You Need to Calm Down" 41, 121
Zuhair Murad 79, 112, 113

PHOTO CREDITS

Cover Photos: John Shearer/TAS23/Getty (*1989, Speak Now, Fearless, Midnights, Reputation*); Kevin Mazur/Getty (*folklore, Red*); Mat Hayward/TAS23/Getty (*Lover*); Taylor Hill/TAS23/Getty (*evermore*)

Interior Photos: John Shearer/TAS23/Getty, 1, 10, 21, 28, 34, 45, 47, 48-49, 55, 76-77, 79, 80, 108, 120, 133, 134, 142, 144, 149, 161, 163, 165, 168, 173, 180; Fernando Leon/TAS23/Getty, 2-3, 35, 52, 86-87; Buda Mendes/TAS23/Getty, 4-5, 22, 40-41, 43, 57, 85, 96, 100, 113, 131, 155, 160, 166, 169, 170-171; Christopher Polk/Getty, 6-7; Mat Hayward/TAS23/Getty, 8-9, 33, 53, 75, 111, 129, 183, 185; Kevin Winter/TAS23/Getty, 11, 36, 56, 106-107, 164, 167, 177, 181; Shutterstock Images, 12-13, 16-17 (maps); TAS2023/Getty, 14-15, 70, 98-99; Taylor Hill/TAS23/Getty, 18-19, 50-51, 59, 71, 112, 136, 139, 148, 174; Emma McIntyre/TAS23/Getty, 20, 37, 46, 94, 103, 121, 122, 143, 178, 179, 187; Grace Smith/MediaNews Group/The Denver Post via Getty Images, 23, 26; Jeff Kravitz/TAS23/Getty, 25, 84, 91, 101, 145, 150; Kevin Mazur/TAS23/Getty, 25, 63, 64, 82, 83, 88, 97, 102, 138, 158, 162; MediaNews Group/Long Beach Press-Telegram via Getty Images, 27; VALERIE MACON/Getty, 29; FREDERIC J. BROWN/Getty, 29; JC Olivera/Stringer/Getty, 30; FOX/Getty, 31; Benjamin B. Braun/Pittsburgh Post-Gazette/ASSOCIATED PRESS, 38-39; Kevin Mazur/Getty, 42, 44, 54, 69, 72, 73, 92-93, 104, 182, 184; Ethan Miller/TAS23/Getty, 58, 154, 157; Octavio Jones/TAS23/Getty, 60, 78, 81, 114, 118, 137, 141; Future Publishing/Getty, 61; Marcelo Endelli/TAS23/Getty, 62, 116, 156; Jessica Christian/San Francisco Chronicle/ASSOCIATED PRESS, 65; Natacha Pisarenko/ASSOCIATED PRESS, 65; Bob Levey/TAS23/Getty, 66, 105; Hector Vivas/TAS23/Getty, 67, 89, 90, 127, 128, 132, 140, 152; Ashok Kumar/TAS24/Getty, 68, 123, 159; Terence Rushin/TAS23/Getty, 74; Lisa Lake/TAS23/Getty, 95, 109; Scott Eisen/TAS23/Getty, 110, 126, 153; Graham Denholm/TAS24/Getty, 115, 125, 147, 186-187; Michael Buckner/Getty, 119; Tom Cooper/TAS23/Getty, 130, 135; Don Arnold/TAS24/Getty, 146, 167; Omar Vega/TAS23/Getty, 151; Natasha Moustache/TAS23/Getty, 172

ABDOBOOKS.COM
Published by Abdo Reference, a division of ABDO, PO Box 398166, Minneapolis, Minnesota 55439. Copyright © 2025 by Abdo Consulting Group, Inc. International copyrights reserved in all countries. No part of this book may be reproduced in any form without written permission from the publisher. Encyclopedias™ is a trademark and logo of Abdo Reference.

Printed in China.
052024
092024

THIS BOOK CONTAINS RECYCLED MATERIALS

Editors: Grace Hansen, Lauri Nelson, Jane Katirgis
Series Designer: Colleen McLaren
Production Designers: Laura Graphenteen, Lori Bye

LIBRARY OF CONGRESS CONTROL NUMBER: 2024936802

PUBLISHER'S CATALOGING-IN-PUBLICATION DATA
Names: Bolte, Mari, author.
Title: Taylor Swift's The Eras Tour encyclopedia / by Mari Bolte
Description: Minneapolis, Minnesota : Abdo Reference, 2025 | Series: Pop culture encyclopedias | Includes online resources and index.
Identifiers: ISBN 9781098287139 (lib. bdg.) | ISBN 9781680769913 (pbk.) | ISBN 9781098276133 (ebook)
Subjects: LCSH: Swift, Taylor, 1989---Juvenile literature. | Concert tours--Juvenile literature. | Popular music--Juvenile literature. | Women in music--Biography--Juvenile literature. | Women singers--United States--Biography--Juvenile literature. | Encyclopedias and dictionaries--Juvenile literature.
Classification: DDC 782.4216409--dc23